UPDATED
Nurturing Parenting Program for Parents and Their Infants, Toddlers and Preschoolers®

Parent Handbook

Stephen J. Bavolek, Ph.D.
Juliana Dellinger-Bavolek, M.S.E.
Illustrations by Cyndee Kaiser

Uniting the World's Families through Nurturing Parenting

Family Development Resources, Inc
Publishers of the Nurturing Parenting Programs
Asheville, North Carolina, Park City, Utah USA
800-688-5822 (Outside U.S. 011-435-649-5822)
www.nurturingparenting.com

CODE: NP2-PHB

4th Edition 2009
3rd Edition 2001
2nd Edition 1988
1st Edition 1985

Copyright by Family Development Resources, Inc.

ISBN # 1-57202-128-4
Printed in the United States of America

The Parent Handbook is designed to be used in conjunction with the 20-part audio-visual series on nurturing parenting. The use of the Parent Handbook and the audio-visual programs as instructional tools is detailed in the Activities Manual for Parents. The Parent Handbook, Activities Manual for Parents and audio-visual programs are component parts of the Nurturing Program for Parents. The Nurturing Program for Parents is recommended for use with the corresponding Nurturing Program for Children.

For more information regarding the Nurturing Program for Parents and Their Infants, Toddlers and Preschoolers, contact::

Family Development Resources, Inc.
1-800-688-5822
email: fdr@nurturingparenting.com

Visit our worldwide web at www.nurturingparenting.com

Table of Contents

About the Authors

Stephen J. Bavolek, Ph.D. is a recognized leader in the fields of child abuse and neglect treatment and prevention, and parenting education. Born and raised in Chicago, Dr. Bavolek's professional background includes working with emotionally disturbed children and adolescents in schools and residential settings, and abused children and abusive parents in treatment programs. Dr. Bavolek has conducted extensive research in the prevention and treatment of child abuse and neglect.

He received his doctorate at Utah State University in 1978 and completed a post-doctoral internship at the Kempe Center for the Prevention and Treatment of Child Abuse and Neglect in Denver, Colorado. He has held university faculty positions at the University of Wisconsin - Eau Claire, and the University of Utah. Dr. Bavolek has received numerous international, national, state and local awards for his work, including induction in 1989 into the Royal Guild of the International Social Work Round Table in Vienna, Austria, and selection in 1983 by Phi Delta Kappa as one of 75 young educators in the country who represent the best in educational leadership, research and services. In addition, he was selected by Oxford Who's Who in 1993 as a member of the elite registry of extraordinary professionals and in 1998 as a member of the elite registry of extraordinary CEO's. Dr. Bavolek was also Mental Health Professional of the Year of Northern Wisconsin in 1985 and Child Advocate of the Year in Utah in 1991. In 1980, he was recognized by the Military Order of the Purple Heart for outstanding research and services to the handicapped.

Dr. Bavolek has conducted thousands of workshops, has appeared on radio and television talk show programs, and has published numerous books, articles, programs and newsletters. He is the principal author of the Nurturing Parenting Programs,® programs which treat and prevent child abuse and neglect, and the Adult-Adolescent Parenting Inventory (AAPI-2), an inventory designed to assess high risk parenting attitudes. Dr. Bavolek is President of Family Development Resources, Inc. and Executive Director of Family Nurturing Centers, International.

Juliana Dellinger-Bavolek, M.S.E. is a parent educator and training specialist with extensive experience in infant mental health, early childhood development, special education and parent education with a focus on parent-infant relationships. For over 32 years, Juliana has worked as an educator with parents of infants and young children. Ms. Dellinger-Bavolek has taught infant massage to families and professionals for over 21 years with the International Association of Infant Massage and Infant Massage USA. She is co-author of Nurturing Touch: Instruction in the Art of Infant Massage.

About the Illustrator

Cyndee Kaiser lives in Eau Claire, Wisconsin and is the mother of three grown children. They are the inspirations for many of the pictures in this book. Along with drawings, Ms. Kaiser is also a muralist and teacher. To see more examples of her work, go to www.cyndeekaiser.com.

Welcome Parents to Nurturing Parenting!

Thank you for your interest and participation in the Nurturing Parenting Program for Parents and their Infants, Toddlers and Preschoolers. We are honored that you have selected Nurturing Parenting as the program to increase your parenting knowledge, understanding and skills. Good choice! You have chosen wisely.

You are now a part of a growing international community of families who have embraced the importance of raising children with respect, compassion and integrity, always keeping the well being of children as the primary goal of parenting. The research from thousands of studies is very clear and persuasive: the way children are treated during the process of their childhood will determine many things: their level of brain development and functioning; their abilities to competently live in an ever increasingly complex and changing world; their personality; the quality of relationships they will have with their peers, children and partners; the contributions they will make to society; and, their overall level of happiness, fulfillment and sense of purpose they will experience in life. Pretty important stuff to remember as you are called in the middle of the night to change a wet diaper or comfort and soothe your baby.

The word nurture means to promote and nourish growth. The primary essence of nurturing forms the primary goal of the Nurturing Parenting Program: to teach parents to promote and nourish themselves, their children and their environment, including animals. To this end, the Nurturing Program addresses five primary issues:

1. **Age Appropriate Expectations and Self Worth.** Promoting growing doesn't just mean kids will get bigger and more capable as they go through their stages of development. Physical health is obviously very important and you will learn information about growth and developmental stages, proper nutrition and immunizations, stimulating your child's brain development, and the differences between male and female brain functioning. You will also learn that critical to raising children are the expectations that parents have for them. Parental expectations send a powerful message to children about their ability to please their parents and to feel a sense of accomplishment. A sense of accomplishment, in turn, feeds a child's perception of him or herself as a capable and giving person. A positive self-worth plays a critical role in childhood success that maintains throughout life. Having appropriate expectations of children is not just an academic awareness of developmental stages. It's greater than that. It's about your child's perception of the word, the people in it, and how all this helps define your child's self-worth.

2. **Responding Empathically to your Child's Needs.** Of all the characteristics of the nurturing parent, empathy is tops on the list. Nurturing is the process of promoting and nourishing growth. Empathy is the ability to respond with caring. Empathy essentially means to be aware of another's needs and to respond in a caring and dignified manner. Being aware of a young child's needs and being responsive in a caring manner is really hard work. The only way empathy can be a constant part of your nurturing parenting practices is by being empathically aware of your own needs and finding time to get your needs met. As a parent you can put your need aside for awhile, knowing you can get those needs met later on in the day. Babies can't do that. That's a skill that comes later when the child's brain functioning is further developed. However, not getting your needs met on a regular basis is going to get old very, very fast. You know the solution: a helping set of nurturing hands to take care of the child while you make time for your self.

3. **Disciplining Children with Dignity.** Discipline means to teach and guide children. It doesn't mean to be harsh and cruel, yelling and hitting, with-holding your love, or threatening them. All these practices are abusive and neglecting and should never ever be a part of discipline. Never ever! Dignity means self-respect: yours and the child's. When a parenting practice is used as a means of guiding children, and that parenting practice damages their self-respect, the entire goal of positive discipline has been lost. What does occur is called negative nurturing. Negative nurturing is promoting all the aspects of childhood that we don't want, but we will get anyway. Positive nurturing is nourishing all the aspects of childhood we do want. The way children are treated during the process of growing up will determine their personality as well as their quality of life.

1

4. **Self-Awareness and Appropriate Family Roles.** Children need to grow up being children. Each developmental stage of growth has requirements that must be met in order to move on successfully to the next developmental stage. At times, children are expected to perform roles in a family that are age-inappropriate. Some examples include young children taking care of their younger siblings; children being confidants or the best friends of their parents. The results are children who take on adult responsibilities. The Nurturing Program that you and your family are participating in will address appropriate family roles by promoting a greater sense of self-awareness. Knowing that children need to be children is the first step in ensuring childhood is a fun, positive time.

5. **Empowering Children and Adults.** The dreaded strong willed child. Ask a parent if their child is strong willed and the comments, facial expressions and groans that you get back appear to suggest, much to their regret, they have a strong-willed child. Actually, parents with strong-willed children are blessed, not cursed even though many parents don't know that. Strong will is called empowerment. Sure, empowered children have opinions and challenge parents. But empowered kids will also challenge their peer group when confronted with engaging in drugs, sex or other potentially harmful or illegal behavior. The level of empowerment achieved by the child will only rise to the level of empowerment achieved by the parents. Power struggles occur when children attempt to go beyond the level of empowerment of the parents. Critical in this issue is enhancing personal power in both the parents and children while developing skills such as cooperation, compromise, negotiation and problem solving.

The nurturing philosophy of parenting is also a philosophy of life that families can embrace to guide the development of their family morals and values. It is within this goal that I am confident that the bonds of your family will grow stronger.

Stephen J. Bavolek, Ph. D

Chapter 1

The Nurturing Program for Parents and Their Infants, Toddlers and Preschoolers

Goal: *To understand the principles of Nurturing Parenting.*

Welcome to the Nurturing Program! Your commitment to improving your parenting skills and the ways you interact with your children is one of the most important actions you will ever take. Nurturing is critical for all families to live in harmony and happiness. To nurture is to promote the growth and development of all of one's positive traits, qualities, and characteristics. To nurture is to respect and care for yourself, for others and for your environment. To nurture is to view the world and all the people, animals and things in it as having value and worth. To nurture is to believe with all of one's heart in the inherent goodness of life. Nurturing is the most powerful characteristic parents can have to promote the positive life of their children.

Did you ever wonder how we learn to become parents? For the most part, young men and women learn about raising children through various informal means. Let's review some of the popular beliefs.

An instinct is an inborn tendency to act in a certain manner. Some people believe that raising children is instinctual and that this ability is brought out when your first child is born. Supposedly, parents are then capable of providing the love, nurturing, skills, and compassion necessary to raise a healthy child.

Not everyone supports the instinctual theory of parenting. Many believe that parenting is a learned behavior that starts very early in our lives. The way we learn how to become parents is a process called "modeling." Modeling means that as parents, we use the same techniques for raising our children that our parents used on us when we were kids.

The experiences we had with our parents probably account for the greater part of our parent training. There are also other factors which have influenced our style of child rearing. Influencing our parenting abilities are the environment we grew up in, our parents' financial statue, the culture or subculture our family was a part of, our ethnic heritage, our race, our religious beliefs, our birth order, and whether we are male or female.

For some of us, the messages we received and the models we watched were mostly positive. These messages gave us a good start in parenting our children. Although there were bad times, the majority of interactions with mom and dad were positive. They left a good impression.

For a lot of us, however, the messages we received and the models we observed were frequently negative. These negative messages resulted in learning inappropriate parenting behaviors. Harsh and abusive parents, experiences, and environments leave a distorted view of what the roles of a child and a parent are all about. Their impact is observed in the countless number of abusive acts committed each year on children, spouses, and the elderly.

What is Nurturing Parenting?

Nurturing Parenting is first and foremost a philosophy that emphasizes the importance of raising children in a warm, trusting and empathic household. It is founded on the belief that a child who is cared for can learn to care for him or herself and can transfer their caring to others and to the environment.

The philosophy of Nurturing Parenting is founded on *seven principles*:

1. **Feelings of Attachment**

   Attachment means a bond between parents and their children. Attached parents convey a deep love to their children that is unconditional. When children feel loved unconditionally, communication, trust, and respect naturally follow.

   In the Nurturing Program parents learn:

   - The importance of establishing nurturing parenting routines for daily times parents and children spend together. These important events are diapering and dressing times, feeding times, bath times, play times and sleep times.

   - Parents also learn the importance of building a warm, cozy, safe home that promotes feelings of closeness.

2. **Empathy**

   Empathy is the ability of parents to put themselves in the place of their children in an attempt not only to recognize their emotions, but also their motives.

   Research tells us that children from empathic homes do better in school, are socially well-adjusted, and are more emotionally stable.

   In the Nurturing Program:

   - Parents and children build their empathic abilities to care for themselves and others.

   - Families focus on establishing structure and discipline and practicing healthy communication patterns.

3. **Nurturing Oneself**

Taking time in getting one's own needs met forms the foundation of understanding and helping children get their needs met. Men and women who continually sacrifice their own needs will soon find themselves feeling burned-out and resentful as fathers and mothers. Nurturing parents take care of themselves, as well as their children.

In the Nurturing Program, parents and children learn:

- To use their personal power to get their needs met.

- To make good choices to enhance their self-worth.

4. **Gentle Touch**

Early and continual parent-child touch has been studied for generations. Children who experience warm and gentle touch develop and maintain healthy relationships throughout their life through a strong and healthy sense of their self.

In the Nurturing Program, parents learn:

- The benefits of massage, while both parents and children learn to use gentle touch in communicating their pleasure and love with each other.

5. **Discipline**

Setting limits through family rules, teaching right from wrong through family morals, and teaching respect and worth through family values are all part of a nurturing family. It is our philosophy that discipline cannot be imposed, beaten into, or forced on a child, but rather develops best by the child modeling parents whose example he or she admires.

In the Nurturing Program, parents and children learn:

- Proven alternatives to hitting, spanking, and yelling as forms of communication and discipline.

6. **Expressing Feelings**

Helping children learn appropriate ways to express their feelings is an important aspect of nurturing parenting. Anger, sadness, and frustration are just as important to express as happiness, love and contentment. Emotional competence helps children and parents stay in control, demonstrate respect, and foster an atmosphere of communication. In the Nurturing Program, parents and children learn:

- Healthy ways to express feelings.

- Appropriate ways to show respect for self, others and their environment.

5

7. Expectations and Self-Worth

Knowing what to expect of children as they reach physical, emotional, and intellectual milestones is important in the development of children's positive self-worth. When parents make demands on children that they are unable to meet, or when they make no demands and have no expectations, children's overall feelings of worth are lowered. In the Nurturing Program parents learn:

- Stages of development and ways to build children's overall self-worth

- The importance of close and stimulating interactions that foster positive brain development.

Self worth Elevator

"Going down!"

Notes and Comments:

Family Home Practice Assignment

1. Hold a family meeting and discuss the word "nurturing" with your children. Help them acquire a meaningful, working definition of the word, and use the word frequently to describe caring situations and actions. Examples:

   "What can we do to nurture our kitty?"

   "What can you do to nurture someone in our family?"

   "What can you do to nurture yourself today?"

2. Review your ratings from the **"Rating My Nurturing Skills"** survey on the next page with your partner. Where are your strengths? Where you your partner's strengths?

3. List three ways you can work on improving your nurturing skills:

   a. _Nurturing myself: sometimes I use the excuse to not to_

   b. _take care of myself._

   c. _Talk to Reagan more.---_

4. Do something to nurture yourself.

5. Spend a minimum of 30-45 minutes each day playing, reading, and or massaging your child(ren).

6

Rating My Nurturing Parenting Skills

Use the chart below to rate your skills at the start and end of your program. Measure how much you have changed!

<u>Directions:</u>

Mark your responses in the columns **Start** when you begin the program. When you complete the program, you will again record your responses in each area in the column marked **End.**

Ratings:

1 = I need lots of improvement.
2 = I need some improvement.
3 = I have average skills in this area.
4 = I have good skills in this area.
5 = I have really good skills in this area.

Rating My Nurturing Parenting Skills

	Start	End
1. Attachment: Having unconditional love for your children	1 2 3 ④ 5	1 2 3 4 5
2. Empathy: Helping your children meet their basic needs	1 2 3 4 ⑤	1 2 3 4 5
3. Nurturing Yourself: Finding time for yourself and taking care of yourself	1 2 3 ④ 5	1 2 3 4 5
4. Gentle Touch: Holding, rocking, touching and massaging your children	1 2 3 4 ⑤	1 2 3 4 5
5. Discipline: Using techniques other than spanking or shouting to teach and guide your children	1 2 3 4 5	1 2 3 4 5
6. Expressing Feelings: Recognizing and expressing your feelings in positive ways	1 2 3 ④ 5	1 2 3 4 5
7. Expectations: Having appropriate expectations for yourself and your children.	1 2 3 4 ⑤	1 2 3 4 5

7

Chapter 2

Nurturing as a Lifestyle

Goal: To increase parents' ability to nurture themselves.

Nurturing is the ability to care. It is a critical skill for all life forms on the planet - especially for humans because they are such complex forms of life. To nurture is to promote the growth and development of all positive traits, qualities and characteristics. To nurture oneself is to treat oneself with caring, kindness, and respect. It is to keep ourselves physically and emotionally healthy, and to make good choices, and to be our own best friend. After all, a best friend can be counted on to be supportive in the bad times and share the good times. Nurturing oneself is a necessary prerequisite to being nurturing parents. How can you care for someone else when you ignore your own needs? It doesn't make sense on paper; it doesn't work in practice.

Why We Don't Nurture Ourselves

Within everyone is the potential to care or to hurt. This potential is fueled, in large part, by the experiences we've had during our lifetime. Inside everyone are four distinct traits of our personality that define who we are and the way we're capable of treating ourselves and others:

- **The Nurturer:** The part of our personality that is capable of giving care, concern and compassion. The care giver we are with our children is our Nurturer.

- **The Nurtured:** The part of our personality that is capable of receiving care, seeking closeness and attachments, and accepting praise and positive touch.

- **The Perpetrator:** The part of our personality that can be cruel, abusive to self and others, is capable of hurting others, and generally disregards the overall goodness and respect of other living things and objects.

- **The Victim:** The part of our personality that believes the hurt and pain given by others is justified and valid. The victim believes the hurt received is for their own good.

A simple way to understand our abilities to nurture or to hurt is to view both abilities on the scale of 1 to 10. A zero (0) represents the complete absence of the behavior. A ten represents the complete presence of the behavior. Imagine both abilities exist on a range of 0 to 10 in frequency (how often) and in severity (to what degree).

Nurturing Parenting

Never	Infrequent	Sometimes	Often	All the Time
0	1 2 3	4 5 6	7 8 ⑨	10

Hurting Parenting

All the Time	Often	Sometimes	Infrequent	Never
10	9 8 7	6 5 4	3 2 1	⓪

The presence of Nurturing Parenting to a high degree (8 or 9) means hurting parenting is at a low degree (2 or 1). The more you're nurturing, the less you're hurting, and vice versa. The goal is to stay nurturing all the time (10) or at the very least, often (9 8 7) and keep hurting out of the picture altogether (0). The reasons are obvious:

If parents practiced nurturing all the time (10) or a high percentage of the time (9 8) children would develop a very "nurtured" part of their personality, and in turn would develop very "nurturing" ways of treating others.

If, however, hurting parenting is practiced often, children develop the "victim" part of their personality and come to believe that being "victimized" is a natural and frequent part of life. Life as a victim gives birth to life as a perpetrator. Perpetrators are those who victimize others. The training to be a perpetrator comes from experience as a victim.

The nurturing philosophy of life and of parenting accepts no degree or frequency of abuse and victimization. The inability of adults to take the time and to make the commitment to nurture themselves is housed in the belief that maybe, just maybe, we don't deserve to be treated with respect all of the time, or maybe we can't expect to live a good life all of the time – that a little victimization now and again helps us appreciate the good times even more.

9

Notes and Comments:

Home Practice Assignment

1. Take time to review your Perpetrator (the person inside you that can and does purposefully hurt yourself or others).

   What do you notice? How do you feel looking at this trait?

   List times your Perpetrator comes out? Do you see any pattern?

2. Now do the same with your Nurturer (the person inside you who can and does purposefully care for others and for yourself.)

   - Review your drawing. Anything come to your attention?

   - Compare your Nurturer and your Perpetrator. What do you notice?

   - Make a list of when you're apt to be the Nurturer. Compare it with the list you made of the times you can act as a Perpetrator.

3. Review the Victim and Nurtured traits of your personality in the same way you did your Perpetrator and Nurturer.

4. When necessary, add or subtract from the lists. Change your drawings as time goes on and notice how you're changing.

5. If appropriate, ask your children or partner to draw their traits. Share your pictures.

6. Spend a minimum of 30-45 minutes each day playing, reading, and/or massaging your child(ren).

Chapter 3

Children's Brain Development

Goal: *To increase parents' knowledge of the importance of positive parent-child interactions.*

* Source: Wisconsin Council on Children and Families, Inc., Madison, Wisconsin.

There is a revolution going on in our understanding of how children's brains develop. Information our parents had has virtually been tossed aside for the recent discoveries in understanding how the brain develops during the first three years of life. Let's look at some recent discoveries and compare them to what we used to believe.

- Old Thinking -
The brains of young children are already fully developed and are waiting to be used.

- New Thinking -
Children's brains are a work in progress. How they develop is up to the experiences they have in their early years.

- Old Thinking -
The genes children are born with (nature) determine how their brains will develop.

- New Thinking -
How children's brains develop depends upon how the genes they're born with (nature) interplay with the experiences they have (nurture).

- Old Thinking -
Children's brains develop as they steadily progress from infancy to adulthood.

- New Thinking -
There are prime times for acquiring different kinds of knowledge and skills called *critical windows*. These critical windows are when certain parts of the brain can learn the best.

How Children's Brains Develop

Each child is born with about 100 billion brain cells, which is ten times the number of stars in the entire Milky Way.

Brain cells are also called *neurons*. These neurons don't touch each other but communicate across a very small space called a *synapse*.

A nerve impulse travels down the neuron and across the synapse to the next neuron.

The nerve impulse travels as an electrical impulse; kind of like the electrical current in the cord of a lamp that lights the light bulb when a lamp is turned on. The electrical impulse in the neuron stimulates the release of chemicals at the nerve end which, in turn, either excites or inhibits the next neuron.

These chemicals are called *neurotransmitters* and are extremely important, especially if they are released in large amounts. Large amounts of neurotransmitters can have a negative effect on the brain's development.

At birth, the connections between the cells are not very fast. But, the more the brain is stimulated, the faster and stronger these connections become. These connections then become a part of the permanent structure of the brain.

But, if the brain is not stimulated, the connections between cells dry up.

Simply, the more connections between the brain cells the better because these connections are forming the structures that will allow a child to learn.

12

Brain Parts

The brain is made up of five major parts:

1. **Brain stem.** The brainstem is fully developed at birth. The brainstem is responsible for functions such as blood pressure, heart rate, and body temperature. The brainstem must be fully functional at birth in order for an infant to survive.

2. **Cerebellum.** The cerebellum controls a person's automatic movements and balance. Dancing, kicking a football, or bringing a cup to the lips to drink are all coordinated by the cerebellum. If a child's cerebellum is damaged, the brain cannot coordinate movement.

3. **Midbrain.** The midbrain controls sleep, arousal responses, appetite and motor movements (such as running and skipping). The midbrain is very important for moving.

4. **Limbic System.** The limbic system controls emotions and long-term memories. The limbic system can override rational thoughts and parts of the brain controlled by the brainstem such as blood pressure. Stress will cause blood pressure to go up. A part of the limbic system is involved in attaching emotions to memory. So, every time we remember an event, the emotion comes along with it. Another part of the limbic system converts information from learning and working into long-term memory. It checks new information against stored experiences in order to establish meaning.

Hypothalamus. The hypothalamus is the part of the limbic system that primes our hormonal responses and is part of the limbic system.

Amygdala. The amygdala handles many emotions and aggressive impulses and is located in the limbic system. The amygdala is larger in males than in females, leading to increases in aggression.

Hippocampus. The hippocampus, also located in the limbic system, is our memory center. It is larger in females than in males.

5. **Cortex.** The cortex is the "executive branch" of the brain. It regulates decision-making and makes judgments about incoming information. The different regions of the cortex are responsible for processing our vision, touch, hearing, speech, language development, and problem solving, and allows us to plan and rehearse our future actions.

Brain Chemicals. There are different brain chemicals that contribute to our growth and development. **Seratonin** is a chemical that calms us down. Males have less seratonin than females. **Oxytocin** is the "bonding" chemical. Higher levels of oxytocin result in higher levels of empathy. The hormone **Testosterone** is the sex and aggression hormone. Males have 20 times more testosterone than females. **Estrogen/ Progesterone** is the female sex hormone.

13

Critical Windows for Babies Brain Development

The term "critical windows" means that at certain times in the life of a child, parts of their brain that are responsible for important functions need to be stimulated so the connections between the brain cells can be made and become strong. The following critical windows for specific functions are presented along with what you can do to build strong brain cell connections.

1. **Vision.**
   Critical Window is Birth to 6 Months

   It is important your child have interesting things to look at. Here are some ideas:

   - Hold your baby so she can look around and see all the wonderful things in her world.

   - Hang mobiles above your baby's bed so he can look at something interesting when he is in his crib or on the floor.

   - Decorate your baby's room with colorful objects. Put up big pictures of animals or of other children's faces for her to look at. High contrast pictures stimulate the brain and strengthen the connections between cells. DO NOT prop your baby in front of a television. The sights and sounds can be an overload for the baby.

2. **Vocabulary and Speech.**
   Critical Window is Birth to 3 Years

   Did you know that an adults' vocabulary is largely determined by the speech that is heard within the first three years? A baby's brain pays attention to the sounds, not the words, that are being said. To build strong neural connections in the brain, here are some suggestions:

   - Talk to your child in full sentences. For example, "Oh, I can see you are a very hungry little girl," is better than "Hungry?"

   - Read, read, read to your children - fun, happy stories with a lot of stimulating pictures.

   - Use an animated voice when talking. Use a fun, high pitched voice.

   - Sing to your baby. She'll love the rhythm and melody of your voice.

When you're with your baby, explain the things you are doing. General conversation is important for your baby even if he can't talk along with you. "Oh what a busy day we have today! First, we have to do the wash, and then we have to go to the grocery store and get all kinds of fun, yummy things to eat. And then..."

3. **Emotional Development.**
   Critical Window is Birth to 18 Months

   A child's home life plays an important role in how a child's personality will develop. A nurturing home will help children grow up emotionally healthy. A home with stress and violence can cause children to become fearful, anxious and hyperactive. Here are some things to do to help your baby develop emotional health.

   - Pick up your baby when he cries. Talk to him. Comfort him. Find out why he's crying. Be nurturing. Your baby really needs to be reassured.

14

- Babies enjoy having the same people in their lives every day. Stick to the same caregiver as much as possible.

- Establish warm, nurturing parenting routines around feeding - both dressing and bed times. Babies love the consistency.

4. **Logic and Math.**
   Critical Window is Age 1 to 4 Years

   Infants begin to become aware of cause and effect, the location of objects, and the function of objects very early in life. Here are some suggestions for helping children develop their reasoning abilities.

   - Explain the purpose of household items. Turn on and off light switches; open and close plastic items; put small plastic bowls into larger ones.

   - Give children things to play with; help them to explore their environment. *Remember: Put safety latches on cabinet doors that contain items that can be harmful to baby. Review your safety checklists and remove dangerous items. Children need to explore in safety.*

Notes and Comments:

Home Practice Assignment

1. Depending on the age of your child, begin doing activities in the **Nurturing Book for Babies and Children** to stimulate your child's brain development. List five things you tried. What was your child's response?

   a. Tell what we did yesterday.

   b. Sing songs in Japanese.

   c. Take him for a walk, feel the fresh air.

   d. Make father & son time.

   e. Read same books (2 books)

2. Do something to nurture yourself.

3. Spend a minimum of 30-45 minutes each day playing, reading, and/or massaging your child(ren).

Reaction:

a. Just listen to me

b. Likes my hands ジェスチャー

c. Likes trees

d. Laugh a lot

e. Likes "Red" color
   try to flip the pages.

15

WHAT EVERY CHILD NEEDS

1. **Interaction**
   Consistent, long-term attention from caring adults actually increases your child's capacity to learn.

2. **Touch**
   Holding and cuddling do more than just comfort your baby - they help his/her brain grow.

3. **Stable Relationships**
   Relationships with parents and other care givers buffer stress that can harm your child.

4. **Safe, Healthy Environments**
   Environments should be free of lead, loud noises, sharp objects, and other hazards.

5. **Self-Esteem**
   Self-esteem grows with respect, encouragement and positive role models from the beginning.

6. **Quality Care**
   Quality care from trained professionals can make the difference when you can't be with your child.

7. **Play**
   Play helps your child explore his/her senses and discover how the world works.

8. **Communication**
   Talking with your baby builds verbal skills.

9. **Music**
   Music expands your child's world, teaches new skills, and offers a fun way to interact with your child.

10. **Reading**
    Reading to your child from the earliest days of life shows its importance and creates a lifelong love of books - and helps grow a healthy brain.

Source: The McCormick Tribune Foundation

Chapter 4

Building Parent-Child Bonding and Attachment

Infants are developmentally very needy young people. In fact, infants are dependent on their parents and other care giving adults for their survival. As adults we often take for granted the basic abilities that allow us to function as capable, independent people. But these same skills and abilities are not yet developmentally available to young children. The result: extreme dependency needs including being protected from harm, being fed, clothed and cleaned, being accepted and loved, being talked to, sung to, read to, and being valued and respected. This basic reliance on parents for survival biologically forms the basis for infants to develop a close and dependent relationship with their parents. Moms, on the other hand, feel a special closeness to their children. This closeness is created by her body chemistry and love which is usually expressed as a strong desire to help children grow, to comfort them and to keep them safe. This mutual feeling of closeness between the parent and the child is called **Bonding**.

Bonding is generally recognized as the period shortly after birth when the baby and parents begin to get to know each other and begin to form a degree of emotional closeness. In many ways, bonding is the continuation of the relationship that began during pregnancy. It is the baby's first relationship in which many professionals suggest establishes the core strengths on which we form future relationships.

Goal: ***To increase parent's awareness of the importance of bonding and attachment with their children.***

17

Ways to Bond with Your Baby

Bonding is generally recognized as the period shortly after birth when the baby and parents begin to get to know each other. In this relationship of love, several things parents can do to build the parent-child bond.

1. **Touch your Baby**. Just after birth, hold your baby. Ask to have the baby lie on your chest, making skin to skin contact and gently stroke your baby's body. Touch your baby's hands, your baby's face. Get to know your baby's body, the palace of your baby's soul.

   Did You Know? Touch is first sense that is developed and the one that is necessary for survival.

2. **Talk to your Baby**. As you are gently touching your baby, talk to her. If you like, sing to your baby. Tell her how proud and happy you are to have her join your family. Tell her all the wonderful things that you have planned for her and the beauty and magic that life brings. Tell her all about the other family members she will meet and who will love her.

   DID YOU KNOW? Babies can recognize their mother's voice from the voices of others and will turn toward their mom when the mom is talking.

3. **Smile at your Baby**. Smiling is an important bonding practice that promotes love and happiness. Smiling communicates your pleasure and reassurance in happy and sad times.

   DID YOU KNOW? The pleasant facial expression that smiling brings can also trigger a smile from your baby.

4. **Look at your Baby**. Make eye-contact. Observe your baby and notice his facial expressions and body postures. Learn your baby's cues. Although your baby can't communicate using words, he certainly is communicating. Notice his sounds, his movements and his facial expressions. These are called **Cues**. What is your baby telling you?

   DID YOU KNOW? Being aware of your baby's cues is called **Attunement**. Being attuned to your baby is a very important function of bonding.

5. **Respecting Baby's Cues.** Being attuned to your baby and her needs, learning how she communicates and feels, and what she might be trying to tell you is the deepest sense of bonding you and your baby can experience. Being attuned to your baby's cues without respecting those cues is not creating a healthy parent-child bond. Respect communicates honor and consideration. When you respond to your baby, do so out of deep respect and honor.

   DID YOU KNOW? Crying is a form of communication. When babies cry they are communicating a need. The manner in which parents respond to their crying child will strengthen or weaken their level of bonding.

6. **Feeding your Baby.** Feeding your baby either with your breast or with a bottle is a very special time to enhance parent-child bonding. During feeding times, touch your baby using gentle touch. Tell him how much you love him. Use a soft voice, smile, make eye-contact, sing songs. Feeding is indeed a special time.

18

Parent-Child Attachment

The bond that begins at birth between the parents and their baby forms a positive and close relationship that continues to develop as the child grows older. This long term bond is called **Attachment**.

The theory of attachment is based on the idea that an infant's first relationship experience usually with the mother shapes the child's social, emotional and cognitive developments. When the mom responds to her child's needs in a sensitive, consistent and nurturing manner, the child receives important messages of "I am here for you, I care about you and you are important to me." These messages are important in forming the emotional basis of trust and security.

Professionals who study the quality of parent-child relationships are quick to note that attached parent-child relationships are very important for positive mental health. According to the New York Attachment Center, early parent-child attachment relationships are essential for five reasons:

- they lay the foundation for our basic ability to trust;
- they serve as a model for future emotional relationships;
- they help develop our ability to regulate arousal, stress and trauma;
- they form our sense of identity, self-worth and competency; and
- they lay the foundation for pro-social morals such as compassion, empathy and conscience.

Attachment Disorders

Children who do not experience an attached, close relationship with their primary caregiver in the first three years of life often develop **Attachment Disorders**. The disorders can range from mild to severe and be expressed in a broad range of symptoms. A common situation leading to attachment disorders is when a birth mom is very needy herself and has little to give her baby. A needy mother giving birth to a developmentally needy baby is a lose-lose situation for both the mom and the child. The child, who depends on mom to get her basic needs met, experiences an emotional form of abandonment because mom has distanced herself while she struggles to get her own needs met.

In many instances, as the child grows older the mother grows increasingly dependent on the child for her basic needs and forms a **Parent-Child Role Reversal**. In this case the mom behaves as the dependent child while her child takes on or is forced to assume the role of the caretaker. As a result the basic feelings of closeness and trust are not fully developed and children express anxious and angry attachments. Their anxiety is based on the fear that they will never be able to experience the normal life of a child. Their anger is directed at their parent who, in the child's eyes, has failed to live up to their part of the relationship which is being the responsible and caring guardian.

19

Children who suffer chronic abuse and neglect in the first three years of life; those who are born to an irresponsible mom who used drugs and alcohol while pregnant; or those children who experience loss of a primary caregiver or persistent changes in caregivers usually experience degrees of attachment disorders.

The most common behaviors associated with attachment disorders include:

- excessive tantrums
- difficulty in self-regulation
- need for control
- defiance
- depression
- manipulation, and
- an inability to experience close relationships

Building Strong Parent-Child Attachments

Attachment is a process of building a close and positive relationship between the parent and the child. Within the first three years, babies are curious about the world around them. This period of curiosity is an ideal time to strengthen the bonds between the parent and the child as well as a critical time to enhance brain development. As mentioned on page 18, being present and responsive to the child's needs is a process called **Attunement**. When parents are attuned to their baby, they engage the child in being a part of and understanding the world they live in.

Here is a list of simple everyday things that parents can do to build a strong and secure parent-child attachment.

- Hold your baby and use gentle touch everyday.

- Learn infant massage strokes and make massage a daily part of baby's day.

- Make eye contact and smile. Children love the feelings of assurance a pleasant face brings. Babies are likely to smile back. It's called mimicking.

- Talk to your child. Describe the color and shape of objects around the house and in the yard. Talk about all you see when traveling in the car or on the bus.

- Read books with colorful pictures. Describe what you see. Tell happy and positive bedtime stories.

- Play with your child. Play is the perfect way to engage your children in learning about themselves and the world they live in.

20

Creativity, fantasies, and imagination are all a part of the world of the child.

- Show interest in your child's day. Get in the habit of asking your child, "And how was your day, sweetie?" When children acquire language skills, you will marvel at their responses. Establishing verbal communication with your children is a perfect expression of attachment.

- Use positive discipline techniques. Avoid harsh and hurtful techniques that are detrimental to your child's overall positive mental health.

- Have appropriate expectations. There is nothing worse than for children to have expectations from parents that they can't meet. Having inappropriate expectations of children is the breeding grounds for feelings of inadequacy and a sense of failure.

Family Home Practice Assignment

1. Review the information in this chapter with other family members. Identify the ways you already build your positive attachment. What are they?

2. Identify the things you can do to increase your positive attachment with your child(ren). What are the additional ways you will build your parent-child attachment?

3. Spend a minimum of 30-45 minutes each day playing, reading, and or massaging your child(ren).

Notes and Comments:

Chapter 5

Ages and Stages:

Having Appropriate Expectations

Nature vs. Nurture

The debate of whether children are more influenced by their genetics (nature) or the way they are parented (nurture) is over. And a long time coming, we might add. From nearly the dawn of modern civilization, anyone and everyone who felt so inclined would engage in the nature vs. nurture argument. Just in case you missed it, the argument would focus on whether children develop good or bad characters because they were born that way (nature) or because they were treated that way (nurture), or in the case of a bad character, the lack of it! Well, after hundreds of thousands of debates over the centuries, professionals on both sides have finally reached a conclusion: we are who we are as a result of the relationship between nature and nurture. In essence, it's not a contest, but a dance.

Goal: To increase parents' awareness of appropriate expectations of children.

Everyone comes into the world with a genetic makeup, or nature. It's theirs and theirs alone. Height, skin color, hair color, gender, and other physical features are the obvious. Temperament, sexual preference, predisposition to alcoholism, to cancer, and to other illnesses are some of the not so obvious that are also a part of us.

They're the gifts our parents give us at conception and, try as we may, there's not much you can do to <u>not</u> be who you are genetically determined to be. But the environment or nurture can influence these predispositions and how, or if, they'll play out.

Developmental Stages

There are four things we know about child development:

1. All children are pre-disposed with certain characteristics but the brain of young children is still developing.

2. All children go through developmental stages with certain tasks and accomplishments needing to be met to move on to the next stage.

3. The expectations parents and other adults have for children grossly affects whether childhood will be a nurturing experience or not.

4. No child is "average" in all areas of growth. Children are unique and each child has their own capabilities. To expect all children in one family to accomplish tasks at the same age is inappropriate.

Why Learn About Developmental Stages?

We learn about developmental stages because we want to become the best parents we can. We also learn about developmental stages because it makes the life of being an infant and a young child easier and happier. Being an infant is not always that pleasant. There are very few things infants can do by themselves besides sleep, cry, wet and soil themselves, and burp. They even have to learn to turnover once they're lying on their backs. It's not simple. Life gets easier as infants get older because they can do more things independently.

But imagine if parents didn't know what infants or children were capable of doing at different times in their lives. Childhood would be a frustrating experience. We might be asking small infants to feed themselves, or young children to set the table, cook the meals, do the dishes. When such inappropriate expectations are placed on children, the children can't complete the task, and they begin to feel badly about themselves.

Developmental Stages and Self-Concept

When we complete a task, no matter if it is a large or small task, we usually feel as if we accomplished something. People often notice our accomplishments and usually praise us for our efforts. The praise we receive helps build in us a positive feeling about ourselves or a positive self-concept.

Trouble begins to occur when we constantly fail to accomplish something. No one recognizes our efforts and we don't receive any praise. In fact, we often receive just the opposite - criticism about how we can't do anything or how bad we are. When this happens often, we begin to believe we can't do anything and begin to feel badly about ourselves. A negative self-concept grows.

The importance of development and self-concept is extremely critical in the growth of children. A self-concept begins very early in life based on how capable we feel we are in pleasing our parents. After all, children want to please the very people they are dependent upon.

When the expectations placed on children or infants are inappropriate, that is, children don't complete the task or do the activity because they are too young and don't have the skills, children see themselves as failures.

Failures are children who can't seem to please mom and dad no matter how hard they try. When mom and dad are not pleased, they don't offer any praise. Without praise from mom and dad, it is nearly impossible for children to feel good about themselves and develop a positive self-concept. Without a positive self-concept, the chances of children trying new tasks or being successful are slim. This failure carries over to school where children will often see themselves as incapable and less bright than the other children.

Primary Areas of Development

There are four primary stages of development all children go through.

1. **Physical Development**

   Physical development means that as children get older, they usually get bigger. Usually when they get older and bigger, their gross motor and fine motor skills increase. Gross motor means activities like running, throwing, jumping, crawling, etc. Fine motor means activities like writing, holding a fork and knife, using scissors, etc. Physical development is important for helping children not only to increase their skills, but also organize their behaviors.

2. **Intellectual Development**

   Intellectual development means that children learn more the older they get. They learn to recognize shapes and colors, recite the alphabet, figure out problems, and many other things. These intellectual abilities continue to increase as children grow older. But stimulation is necessary in order for these intellectual capabilities to occur. Without stimulation, these capabilities may lag behind or fail to develop.

3. **Language Development**

   Language development means that as children grow older, their communication skills increase. Their ability to use words, phrases, and sentences in writing and in conversation helps them gain mastery of their environment by expressing their needs and understanding the needs of others. Language expands from a few simple sounds during the first year of life, to the use of thousands of words in their teen years. Talking to children when they're babies and continuing good commination skills throughout childhood is an essential quality of nurturing parenting.

4. Social and Emotional Development

Social and emotional development go hand-in-hand. The way we treat children and the care they receive affect the way they mature, and are capable of interacting with others. Children's emotional growth goes from an early stage of dependence and taking to a later stage of independence and giving.

In this area, the ability for a child to use their physical, intellectual, and language skills to the best of their abilities and in positive ways hinges on how well children develop socially and emotionally.

What is Important to Learn

Listed in the following pages is information about developmental stages that you should know. Having a good working knowledge of what your children can or can't do will help you in having appropriate developmental expectations of your children. In turn, you will encourage your children to meet success and reinforce positive feelings about themselves.

Developmental Summaries

The developmental summaries of children, located in the next chapter, serve as a rough guide to normal child development. It should be noted that the lists serve only as a summary and are not a complete index of all the things children can do at any given stage. Children born with birth problems such as prematurity, low birth weight, or illness may not be able to do the things that other children can do who didn't have problems at birth. Most likely, such children will be behind and will need more time to catch up. Only with the support of their family will children with special developmental needs, grow to the fullest of their capabilities.

Family Home Practice Assignment

1. List at least one short-term expectation you have for your child:

   _____

   _____

   _____

   _____

   _____

   _____

   _____

2. List one long-term expectation you have for your child.

   _____

   _____

   _____

   _____

   _____

   _____

3. Spend a minimum of 30 ro 45 minutes each day playing, reading, and/or massaging your child(ren).

Notes and Comments:

25

Chapter 6

Ages and Stages:

Infancy
Birth to One Year

Goal: To increase parents' awareness of children's abilities.

The first year of an infant's life is both fascinating and startling. For years, psychologists have thought that babies were incompetent creatures who were unable to comprehend the world around them. Today we know that is untrue. At six to ten days, the newborn can recognize the mother by her smell. Some studies reveal that newborns can move their bodies in rhythm to the meaningful speech of adults. Babies at two weeks will look at their own mothers more frequently than they will look at strangers. It is apparent that very young infants can begin to make some sense of their new environment. As they grow older during their first year of life, their body language, intelligence, and social interactions also increase.

26

Physical Development

The major part of the infant's first year is devoted to survival. The infant is completely helpless at birth and is totally dependent upon the parents for help. Being fed, held, touched, looked at, and talked to have significant impact on the growth of the child. There is so much activity that the average baby sleeps from 16 to 20 hours each day. In fact, there is so much going on during the first year that it is impossible to notice everything. The first year is indeed an important one for the child's physical growth.

- Automatic reflexes such as hand-to-mouth (0-2 months)

- Can focus on objects 8 - 15 inches away (newborn)

- Makes cooing, crying, and grunting sounds (newborn)

- Will use eyes to follow you (2 months)

- Will lift head when on stomach (2 months)

- Sucks fingers (2 months)

- May be pulled slowly by hands to a sitting position (2 months)

- May be starting to teethe (4 months)

- Can sit up without support for a short time (7 months)

- Can begin to crawl by pulling self forward with arms and dragging legs and stomach (7 months)

- With help of furniture, can pull self up to stand (7 months)

- Likes to pick things up and drop them, only to pick them up again (7 months)

- Feeds self pieces of food with hands (7 months)

- Starts practicing walking but continues crawling (10 months)
- Likes to eat meals using fingers, begins using one hand more than the other (10 months)

- Begins a tottering walk with legs wide apart (12 months)

- Sits independently on hard surface (12 months)

Intellectual Development

Physical and intellectual development are closely related to one another. The child learns about the world through exploration of objects, by moving around, and through interactions with the parents. Jean Piaget, a Swiss psychologist, helped us understand how children learn. He believed that intelligence involves adaptation to the world. Such adaptation means that the individual is capable of interacting effectively with the environment. The behavior of infants during the first year, and subsequent years, is to help them understand, adapt, and interact effectively with their world.

- The language of a newborn is crying. Crying occurs without tears for a special reason: to have needs met (0 - 2 months)

- Reflex behaviors, like sucking, are practiced (0 - 2 months)

- Begins to recognize familiar voices or faces (2 months)

- Responds to strangers by crying or staring (2 months)

- Likes repetition of simple acts like sucking, open and closing hands, etc. for own sake of activity (2 - 3 months)

- Baby still cries but also laughs out loud (4 months)

- Can imitate sounds; watches your mouth with interest when talking (7 months)

- Child repeats an act to observe change in the environment. Baby kicks mobile to make it go. However, actions are not organized with a purpose; the goal is discovered accidentally in the process of activity (6 - 8 months)

- Follows moving objects with eyes (1 - 2 months)

- Child uses responses to solve problems and to achieve some goal. For example, a child may move one object to get at another (12 months)

- Responds to and imitates facial expressions of others (5 - 12 months)

Language Development

Language develops very slowly during the first year of life. At birth, babies cannot say anything. By the end of their first year, the vocabulary increases to about two to eight words. ***An adult's vocabulary is largely determined by the speech they heard in the first three years of life. The first two years are the most important.***

Babies, however, do communicate their needs even without language. Crying is a way babies let their parents know they are either wet, hungry, tired, or frightened. Mothers and fathers soon learn the difference between a cry of fear and one of hunger. By the second month, babies begin cooing - a way of showing their pleasure. Babbling begins during the fourth or fifth months. Syllables are repeated over and over again. Parents who talk to their babies, and praise and reinforce their efforts at communication, help facilitate the development of language.

- Responds to speech by looking at speaker (0 - 12 months)

- Makes crying and non-crying sounds (0 - 12 months)

- Babbles by repeating some vowel and consonant sounds (0 - 12 months)

- Attempts to imitate sounds (0 -12 months)

- Babies begin to "understand" many words or phrases such as "No, Come, Bring," etc. (12 months)

28

Social/Emotional Development

The stages of social and emotional growth are described by Erik Erickson. In the earliest stage, birth to one year, the child struggles with learning to trust or mistrust himself and others in his environment. The degree to which a child comes to trust the environment, other people, and himself, depends to a considerable extent upon the quality of the care the child receives.

The child whose needs are met, whose discomforts and fears are quickly removed, who is held, loved, played with, and talked to develops a belief that the world is a safe place, and that people are dependable and helpful.

The child who receives inconsistent and inadequate care and who is rejected develops a basic mistrust of others, his environment, and self. For this child, the world is not a safe, fun place to be and people are not to be depended upon to have needs met.

Although the child is actively involved in developing trust or mistrust in the first year, the same issue arises again at each successive stage of development.

- Likes high-pitched voices and will usually quiet down when they hear them (0 - 2 months)

- Smiles spontaneously (0 - 2 months)

- Loves to be played with and likes to be picked up (4 months)

- Responds differently to strangers (may cry) than to familiar persons (4 -6 months)

- Babies may give joyful kicks and gurgle and laugh to engage mother in play (5 months)

- Knows that mother exists even though she may not be visually present (5 months)

- May become attached to a particular toy; play time is important (7 months)

- Child is beginning to learn to be independent. May go a little away from you, but will quickly return (10 months)

- Child will express frustration (through crying) for failure to master some task (8 - 10 months)

- Child loves an audience and will repeat any behavior that gets it (12 months)

- Tantrums may occur. Based on needs and limited abilities, a child may desire to have or do something that cannot be achieved (12 months)

This is our great nightmare as parents. Later on in the program we'll discuss how to handle tantrums. For now we'll just say that children learn how to handle their frustrations sooner when we are understanding and know how to continuously support them in their emotional development.

Family Home Practice Assignment

1. List a behavior that you have observed in your child in each of the four principal areas of development.

   - Physical: _____

     _____

     _____

     _____

     _____

   - Intellectual: _____

     _____

     _____

     _____

     _____

   - Verbal: _____

     _____

     _____

     _____

     _____

   - Social/Emotional: _____

     _____

     _____

     _____

     _____

2. List one long-term expectation you have for your child.

3. Spend a minimum of 30 to 45 minutes every day playing, reading or practicing nurturing touch with your child(ren).

Copyright 2009   Family Development Resources, Inc.   www.nurturingparenting.com   1-800-688-5822

Chapter 7

Ages and Stages:

Toddler
One Year to Three Years

**Goal: *To increase parents'
awareness of children's
abilities.***

Life with toddlers is rarely dull. Their busyness, intensity, curiosity, independence, and increasing verbal skills make them both exciting and frustrating for parents. Parents are often pleased by some of the observations they verbalize, and sometimes outraged at their stubbornness.

This stage has often been called the "terrible twos" because of the child's increased needs to explore the surroundings and gain control over the environment. Both expressive language and physical mobility increase during this stage. The toddler is in a rush to discover a new style of living.

31

Physical Development

By the end of the first year, the average one-year-old is between 27 to 29 inches in height and weighs approximately 22 pounds. By the end of the third year, height has increased to around 36 inches and weight to 35 pounds. Although growth in the second and third years is slower than infancy, it still occurs at a rapid pace.

Large Muscle Development (Gross Motor)

- The child should be walking better. Feet are more parallel and can walk without holding arms up for balance. Child usually can walk backwards (15 months)

- The toddler can pick up things from a standing position without falling. Now that hands are free, he loves to carry things, especially big things (15 - 18 months)

- Child likes to push or pull toys; loves to throw things (15 - 18 months)

- Seats self in child's chair; moves to music (18 - 24 months)

- Runs, jumps, climbs, and stands on chair, walks upstairs, crawls downstairs backwards, kicks at ball, loves pounding, tugging, lugging, dumping (18-24 months)

- Climbs small ladder (around 36 months)

- Walks on tiptoes; stands on one foot with aid (24 - 36 months).

Small Muscle Development (Fine Motor)

- Combines use of several objects: hitting one object with the other; dropping small things into large containers (15-18 months)

- Begins to use spoon to eat; drinks from a cup that is held (18 months)

- Turns several pages at a time; can make a straight stroke with pencil or crayons instead of just a scribble (18 months)

- Can turn a doorknob, builds tower of many blocks (18 months)

- Turns single pages; drinks from a cup without help (24 - 36 months)

- Removes shoes, pants, socks, sweater, unzips large zipper (24 months)

- Snips with scissors; holds crayons with thumb and fingers, not fists; paints with wrist action; makes dots, lines, circular strokes (24-36 months)

- Uses one hand consistently in most activities (24 - 36 months).

Intellectual Development

The increased exploration and discovery of objects within the environment leads to activities that expand the child's understanding of the world. At eighteen months, the toddler's interest is directed beyond his body. Toddlers begin to understand that each object has an independent existence and permanence. Such understanding leads to exploration of these objects and how they work. The child learns that a chair remains the same whether seen from above, behind, or underneath.

From eighteen months to two years of age, children are limited to the immediate experiencing of objects, people, and whatever or whoever else is present at the moment. A lot of time is spent staring at objects and people. The beginning of language use and memory occurs around two years. By three, children are able to remember events, people, and activities they observed in the environment. Memory expands dramatically. Memory helps in the development of language. During two and three years of age, language develops rapidly, and imaginative and imitative play increases. Parents are often surprised at what children are able to remember and imitate later.

- Toddlers are curious about textures. They like to stroke a cat or dog and rub their cheeks against the fur (18 months)

- Imitates actions and words of adults (18 - 24 months)

- Toddlers are attracted to water and to toilets and enjoy playing in the bathroom (18 - 24 months)

Recognizes difference between you and me (18 - 24 months)

- Has limited attention span; accomplishes primary learning through exploration of environment (12 - 24 months)

- Responds to simple directions, "Give me the block," " Get your shoes" (24 - 36 months)

- Recognizes self in mirror; can talk briefly about what he is doing (24 - 36 months)

- Has limited sense of time: vaguely knows idea of past and future and knows such terms as "yesterday" and "tonight," although they may be used incorrectly (24 - 36 months)

Language Development

Babies begin to produce a few basic words at about a year of life. By 24 months, most children are speaking phrases and have a wide range of words. A two-year-old has a vocabulary of perhaps 50 words, which increases to about 900 words by the time the child is three.

Many factors contribute to the development of language in a child. A strong, emotional relationship with mother, enhanced by the amount and quality of time spent together, and the amount of talking, asking questions, and responding to what the child says increases the child's verbal activities.

33

- Says first meaningful words (12 - 24 months)

- Uses single word plus a gesture to ask for objects (12 - 24 months)

- Refers to self by name; uses "my" or "mine" to indicate possession (12 - 24 months)

- Toddler likes to talk to self; replaces baby language with sentences; likes to repeat words (24 months)

- Joins words together in two-word phrases, e.g. "See doggy" (24 months)

- Asks what and where questions (24 - 36 months)

Social/Emotional Development
Autonomy vs. Doubt

Parents of toddlers have an overwhelming job. The child continues to be needy and dependent, but at the same time is growing and developing into an independent person both physically and emotionally. The second and third years of a child's life focus on the emergence of autonomy. This autonomy is built upon the child's new motor and mental abilities. The child takes pride in his new accomplishments and wants to do everything himself. Whether it is pulling the wrapper off a piece of candy, wanting to dress himself, or flushing the toilet, the child wants to

demonstrate his competence at completing the task.

The importance of this stage reflects upon the willingness of parents to allow the child to express autonomy. If parents are impatient and do for the child what the child is capable of doing, they create a sense of shame and doubt. Overprotecting, abusive treatment, criticizing, and inappropriate expectations foster feelings of "I'm not capable" or "I'm not worthy." Such doubt or shame will handicap a child's attempts to achieve autonomy in adolescence and adulthood.

Parents need to help a child explore and grow during this stage. To accomplish this task, parents can:

- **Provide a safe environment for the child to explore.** "Child proof" the house. Remove breakables and eliminate hazards.

- **Provide a creative environment for the child to explore.** Use creative toys and games to facilitate learning.

- **Be involved in the child's exploration.** Talk to the child to reinforce natural curiosity and exploration of the environment.

Problems

Special social/emotional problems arise during this time that will be briefly discussed

34

Separation From Parents

Children quite frequently get upset at separation from the parents, particularly from mother. The emotional tie that is developed between mother and child results in the child wanting to be with the parent. Crying at separation is normal. Throwing temper tantrums at separation is a sign of possible problems.

Research has shown that children who are positively attached to their mother develop a sense of trust and feelings of security. Securely attached toddlers are outgoing preschoolers who are well-liked, attack new problems vigorously and positively, and can accept help from others. They are sympathetic to others, self-directed and goal-oriented, and exhibit high self-esteem and self confidence.

Toddlers who are not positively, emotionally attached to the parents, particularly to the mother, exhibit problem behaviors. Such children are anxious, throw more tantrums when presented with problems, are more negative in response to mother, ignore and oppose her in many ways. Children who feel less securely attached to mom fear separation. The fear can turn into panic during actual separation. To minimize the fear, a strong attachment needs to be established between mother and child. Feelings of security need to be developed, and assurances that mother will not abandon the child need to be expressed.

Assertiveness

As the toddler becomes more aware of self, more independent, more definite in what he can and cannot do, the child will become more assertive in interactions with parents and peers. "No" becomes a common word. "I want," I

need," and "More" are other phrases and words frequently expressed in the toddler years. Children also like to command parents, sometimes adopting dictatorial tones of "Do this" or "Do that!"

Assertion turns to frustration and anger when toddlers cannot accomplish what they set out to do. When parents exert limits (discipline) designed to manage behavior, toddlers may express their anger physically - yelling, crying, temper tantrums, holding breath, or throwing objects. The physical activities release the tension that cannot be expressed in words. Consistent application of ignoring undesirable behavior, praising desirable behavior, and punishing unacceptable behavior through time-out, loss of privilege, etc. will help toddlers negotiate this stage of development. As children become more capable and competent at achieving their ends, the tantrums will decrease.

Toilet Training

Most experts agree that somewhere between 18 to 24 months, children are ready to learn toilet training. *However, it is important for parents to know that, just like eating, toileting is an area that parents cannot control, and the first area children learn that they can control. Therefore, in an extreme struggle of wills in toilet training, the child will win.* An approach that helps children lessen their need to control this area is generally more successful. Several hints are offered:

35

1. **Three guidelines exist for determining a child's readiness for toilet training:**

   - **Bladder control** - the ability to stay dry for several hours.

   - **Physical Readiness** - the ability to get to the toilet and pull pants down.

   - **Instruction Readiness** - the ability to understand instructions and communicate needs.

2. **Don't make a big deal out of toilet training.** Don't talk about it much, or give it much praise. Children can use the achievement to frustrate parents if they get angry.

3. **Establish a toilet routine.** There are many books available on how to establish such a routine.

4. **Use a potty chair. It is less frightening than a toilet.**

5. **Have the child observe the parent or sibling in the bathroom as a model.**

For more information on **Potty Training**, read **Chapter 40** in this Handbook.

Family Home Practice Assignment

1. List a behavior that you have observed in your child in each of the four principal areas of development.

   - Physical: _____

     _____

     _____

     _____

     _____

   - Intellectual: _____

     _____

     _____

     _____

     _____

   - Verbal: _____

     _____

     _____

     _____

     _____

   - Social/Emotional: _____

     _____

     _____

     _____

     _____

2. List one long-term expectation you have for your child.

3. Spend a minimum of 30 to 45 minutes every day playing, reading or practicing nurturing touch with your child(ren).

Chapter 8

Ages and Stages:

Preschool
Three Years to Six Years

Goal: *To increase parents'
awareness of children's
abilities.*

The preschool period in a child's life is an exciting time. During this time, the child reaches out to the world beyond their home. For them, the world is an exciting place with many things to do, to touch, to experience, and to eat. Although the preschool child cannot read or write, or compute logical processes, the quest for knowledge overrides any developmental limitations. The preschool years set the stage for experiences, friends, and accomplishments obtained outside the home.

Physical Development

In comparison to earlier stages of development, the physical growth of the preschool child has slowed down considerably. Nevertheless, preschoolers usually gain 2 ½ to 3 inches in height each year, and three to five pounds in weight. The physical growth of the brain achieves about 90% of its adult size around the age of five years.

The growth of the brain facilitates control of voluntary movements. Old skills are refined and elaborated, and are put to new use. The basic motor abilities are present.

Large Muscle Development
(Gross Motor)

- Takes longer steps when running or walking (5 years)

- Catches large ball (4 - 5 years)

- Skips on one foot (4 - 5 years)

- Hops on one foot (4 - 5 years)

- Many can broad jump 28 to 35 inches (5 - 6 years)

Small Muscle Development
(Fine Motor)

- Children can draw, use scissors, and begin to color (4 - 6 years)

- Can get close to drawing a person (5 years)

- Can begin to read, write (5 - 6 years)

- Copies shapes - can draw square and triangle, probably not a diamond (5 - 6 years)

- Can paint with broad strokes (5 - 6 years)

Intellectual Development

Preschoolers are intellectually curious and actively seek to learn as much about their environment as they possibly can. The child learns to represent objects, persons, and perceptions with symbols. It is the beginning of functional language. The child is no longer tied to what is physically present.

Questions begin during the preschool years, first about the names of objects and activities, then about the purpose of routines. Increased questions, dreams, nightmares, and fantasy in play are all indications of advances in intellect.

During the preschool period, children believe everything exists for a purpose, even themselves. As such, the child's questions usually reflect such interest: 'Mommy, why is there rain?" Where do babies come from?" Where was I before I was born?" "Do I have to die?" Answer such questions in terms of purpose or function. "It rains to make the trees and flowers grow." "Babies come from mommies." "Before you were born, you were just a thought with your mommy and daddy." "We all get old and eventually have to die." When children receive a response that suggests a function or purpose, they are usually satisfied.

Preschool children have limited concepts of things and only pay attention to a small number of characteristics. For example, if they see water poured from a short fat glass into a tall thin one, the child will say there is more water in the tall one, even though no water has been added. Preschoolers cannot easily understand relational terms such as "longer" or "smaller" unless the objects compared are very different.

Language Development

Preschool children are active conversationalists. As they develop intellectually, their language usage increases.

- Vocabulary of about 900 words at three years; 2,000 words at five to six years

- By the age of five years, children use complete sentences strung together with conjunctions.

- Although they speak clearly, children will have problems with pronunciation and stuttering. These problems are usually temporary and a normal part of development.

- They experiment with sounds, often making up rhyming words (3 - 6 years)

- Uses "because, how, why" in their efforts to interpret cause and effect (4 - 6 years)

- Conversations tend to be one-sided (4 - 6 years)

- Children love to giggle with "toilet talk," i.e. words such as "poo poo, pee pee," etc. It's not until later years that children learn to adapt conversation to suit the company.

Social/Emotional Development

Preschoolers are highly social beings. They are ready to reach out and interact with other children in a more responsive fashion. A sense of self as a person; an "I" who thinks, feels, and acts is ready to interact in a more assertive way with their environment.

Initiative vs. Guilt

The social dimension that appears during this stage is initiative, at one pole, and guilt, at the other. Children initiate activities due mainly to their gaining mastery of their abilities. This holds true for motor, language, and play activities.

Whether the child will leave this stage with a sense of initiative or sense of guilt depends to a considerable extent on how parents respond to self-initiated activities. Children who are given freedom to initiate motor, language, and play activities have their sense of initiative reinforced.

On the other hand, if children are made to feel their motor activities are bad, questions are a nuisance, and play is silly or stupid, guilt over self-initiated activities will develop that could persist through later life stages.

Play/Imaginary Friends

By age five, children can play cooperatively in a small group. When children aren't available to play with, they invent imaginary companions to fill the void. Imaginary friends are fairly common beginning around age three. Children who have imaginary companions are often bright, creative, verbal, more cooperative, and more aggressive than children who do not. The existence of imaginary friends suggests that children generate the kinds of experiences they need for their own development that the environment cannot provide.

Sex Roles and Identify

Most preschoolers play with both boys and girls but by age six prefer friends of their own sex. Girls imitate their mothers; boys try hard to act like men.

Nighttime Wetting

Children usually have learned to be potty trained around three years of age. However, accidents can happen and do, usually at night.

Nighttime wetting is more common among boys than girls, largely due to the fact that the nervous system of boys matures more slowly. Ask the child how he thinks the problem could be solved. Some possible solutions are not drinking liquids after dinner, going to the bathroom just before bedtime, or not changing the sheets until morning. Again, the parents should remain supportive and give the child encouragement. Scolding or punishing will not solve the problem.

Excessive Masturbation

Although masturbation is a normal behavior, excessive masturbation can be a concern. Excessive masturbation may be the result of an unhappy, anxious child. Finding the sources of the unhappiness and anxiety, and correcting them, is the first step.

Often excessive masturbation in children results from not being a part of a social group. Providing many opportunities for activities with peers, helping the child achieve feelings of competence, and parental support often ends the problem.

Fears

Fears are a natural part of growing up. During the preschool years, children often fear animals, dark, imaginary creatures, and natural events like storms, fires, thunder, and lightening.

Parents who criticize a child for his fears, who are sarcastic or even punish a child for having fears, are not helping to reduce the fears. These tactics only tend to decrease the self-confidence and self-esteem of the child. A model of confident, non-fearful behavior, discussion of the fear, support, and understanding from the parents helps the child to understand the fear and eventually diminish the fear to a more manageable level.

40

Family Home Practice Assignment

1. List a behavior that you have observed in your child in each of the four principal areas of development.

   - Physical: _____

     _____

     _____

     _____

     _____

   - Intellectual: _____

     _____

     _____

     _____

     _____

   - Verbal: _____

     _____

     _____

     _____

     _____

   - Social/Emotional: _____

     _____

     _____

     _____

     _____

2. List one long-term expectation you have for your child.

3. Spend a minimum of 30 to 45 minutes every day playing, reading or practicing nurturing touch with your child(ren).

Chapter 9

Ages and Stages:

School-Age
Six to twelve years

Between the ages of six to twelve years, children have gained control of their physical and social behavior and language. They can express themselves easily, and can take care of many of their own needs. Children have new experiences and new friendships that are outside of the family. Depending on communication patterns established in earlier years, many children 6 to 12 years will share their experiences if the parents are willing to listen.

The abilities acquired before age six are now put to new use. Establishing friends in school largely depends on previous learning and interactions with parents in early childhood. Recess time and exercise are really important for children of both genders. Academic achievements depend greatly on previous learning and interactions had with parents during the first years of childhood.

Goal: ***Increase parents' awareness about children's abilities.***

Socially, children should have broken the strong dependency ties with mom, in order to achieve more satisfying relationships with friends. Children learn during this period, to deal with success and failure; to defend themselves from bullies and how to interact with other adults.

Although these years are socially, intellectually, and emotionally rewarding, children face many seemingly insurmountable and catastrophic crises.

Physical Development

From ages 5 to 10 years, boys and girls, have approximately the same height, weight and physical measurements. At 5 years of age, they reach a height of 3 feet 5 inches and around 45 pounds in weight. By age 10, they are 4 ft 6 inches high and weigh around 75 to 80 pounds. At this age the growth patterns of boys and girls start to change. Girls begin to mature physically more rapidly than boys. The development of breasts, broadened hips, smaller waist and the onset of menstruation all contribute to a sensitivity girls have about their bodies. Remarkably, boys and girls who will have the same adult height can be up to 7-8 inches apart at his age. Boys begin to catch up physically to girls around 13. Such differences in development can cause problems for early maturing girls and late maturing boys.

Early and Late Maturation

Neither peer group can effectively deal with the early and late bloomer. Girls seem to have more difficulties with their peers when they mature earlier than boys do. Early maturation in girls seems to heighten interest in dating at a time when other boys and girls their age have little or no interest in dating. As such, she doesn't seem to fit in with her peers and is often rejected. She seeks the company of older friends who find her physically mature but socially immature and also end up rejecting her.

Early maturing boys on the other hand, are more accepted. Their physical prowess in athletics is valued. Boys that mature more rapidly are generally very popular. Late maturing boys, however, are perceived as childish because of their physical size. To be accepted they usually act like clowns for their peers to notice and respect them. A poor self concept is usually the result of early maturing in girls and the result of late maturing in boys.

Intellectual Development

The 6 to 12 year old possess many more mental abilities than the preschooler. These abilities help them to reason with more logically and learn new ideas. *All learning is sequential and in large part, the child falls back on the skills learned as a preschooler to acquire new skills.* Early learning plays an important role in this stage.

At around 6 years, Piaget, a noted specialist in child development, suggests that children are able to figure out problems and give reasons for what they think. But the thoughts offered are usually based upon what was observed. At about age 7, the child will be able to figure out that the tall skinny glass holds the same amount of water as the short, fat glass.

At around age 12, the child expands his ability to think logically. He can draw conclusions, test ideas and think of possible alternatives to problems. All these skills are necessary for a child to gain mastery in learning related activities presented in school.

Language Development

Language is a tool for communication for the 6 to 12 year old. Vocabulary grows steadily each year. Sentence structure, grammar and meanings of words are skills the child continues to develop and use.

43

Social/Emotional Development

Industry vs. Inferiority The importance of the emotional development of a 6 to 12 year old focuses on the child's sense of industry at one end and inferiority at the other end. According the Erickson, industry refers to the child's never ending curiosity of how things are made, how they work and what they do. When parents encourage a child to make, do, or build practical things, be it a little toy house or car, and reward their efforts, a sense of industry is enhanced. However, when children's efforts at doing or making something or making something are discouraged or ridiculed, a sense of inferiority is developed. As we will discuss a little later, a sense of self is largely dependent on the qualities of industry or inferiority.

The concepts of industry and inferiority are important when considered in relation to school. A child's school experiences influence which of the two qualities will be enhanced. Up to now, parents were largely responsible for the emotional growth of the chilled. During the elementary school years, the actions of teachers, administrators, and peer groups reinforce either industry or inferiority.

Peers

Perhaps the most important source of social contact is the child's peer group. They establish deep attachments, express their thoughts and share experiences with friends. It is during these years that children join groups and organized athletics to enhance their social contacts. Boy Scouts, Girl Scouts, Brownies, etc. are popular neighborhood groups. Swimming, Little League; soccer, basketball etc. are sporting activities that are organized around team participation. As children participate in group activities they are able to test their skills and form some sense of their own abilities.

Parents

The role of the parents changes from direct providers to facilitators of social contact. It is during this development stage that most parents spend their time driving their son or daughter from one activity to another.

Children up to the age of 7 or 8 often regard their parents as perfect. It is at this stage where children learn that parents can be wrong. They begin to challenge rules, doubt parental advice, and question parental wisdom. Although parents are not considered all knowing and powerful, children still see them as helpful and caring.

Self

Children at the initial part of the elementary school year stage perceive themselves in terms of physical qualities and material possessions. When asked to tell about themselves, a typical response might be, "I am tall, skinny, have blond hair and a new video game." With increasing age, children begin to think of themselves in reference to their personality. "I am shy, helpful and sometimes I lose my temper."

The sense of self develops largely from relationships with their peers, and from their ability to start and accomplish things (industry). How others view and interact with the child, at this stage often dictates how the child perceives themselves. The establishment of a self-worth based on the interactions with others leads to interesting relationships. Short-term friendships, gangs or in-groups and group conformity are typical to a child in this stage.

The physical, intellectual, and skill competencies of a 6 to 12 year old also contribute to a sense of self-worth. Erickson emphasizes that wanting to make things and to accomplish things, a sense of industry, is important to the development of a positive perception of self. Feelings of inferiority, the result of not being encouraged by parents to make things, participate in activities with peers, and learn new skills will affect the child in later stages of development.

Concern and Problem Areas

Homework. Typically, the majority of 6 to 12 year olds do not like to study at home or do homework. Because of this, the issue of homework tends to become a battleground between parents and children.

44

There are few things in a child's life that conjure up feelings of dread, disappointment and anger than the task of having to dos school work at home. Homework- the curse of children and parents alike. It is not surprising that children, parents, educators and researchers all debate the value of homework and whether it has a positive or negative impact on children's school performance. Before discussion on how to help children deal with this issue, let's examine the facts and opinions of homework.

1. Research studies examining the benefits of homework generally conclude it has little to no positive influence on children's school performance in the elementary school level. At the middle and high school levels, given in moderation, homework can have a positive impact.

2. Most homework is dull, boring repetitive tasks that review what was already taught. Homework that invites creative application of learned concepts has a more positive benefit.

3. Adults resent having to do work related to their job after work hours. After work, adults wish to use their home time to relax. Children, on the other hand, are required to do what the majority of adults resent – working at home.

4. In moderation, homework which uses creative application can be enjoyable. In abundance, it robs children of leisure time, creates stress in the family, takes away from family time, and builds a sense of "workaholism" (being addicted to work)

If work time is having detrimental effect on your child and family, meet with you child's teacher and share your concerns. A polite and informative discussion might be looked upon as favorable and could solve this problem.

Here are some suggestions to help reduce conflicts in this problem area:

1. Encourage your children to do their homework assignments, offer them a quiet place to study, and books and ideas that can help them do it. Show interest in what they are studying and discuss it often.

2. Provide them with enrichment opportunities, like visits to the museum or the library.

3. Children are the one with homework, not their parents. Offer them a reward to encourage them to do their homework or take away a privilege when they do complete their work but only when absolutely critical. Nevertheless, you should not always offer them direct assistance. It is important that they learn to work independently.

4. If your children do not finish their homework, as hard as it might be for you, they will have to suffer the consequences. Their future motivation for finishing homework could be based on the consequence they suffered the first time they did not complete it.

Peer Group

Another "bone of contention" between parents and children can be the peer group: characters the parents don't approve of being called "friends" by their children. In some cases children are sometimes attracted to what appears to be their opposites. Withdrawn kids might be attracted to more 'acting out" ones primarily for intrigue. Typically, these friendships won't last as both realize there is little between them that is common.

Some general suggestions for peer groups are:

1. Invite your son or daughter to bring their friends home. Make your home the gathering spot.

2. Meet the parents of your children's friends. Form your perceptions from experience and not from heresay.

3. At this age, a lot of kids have sleep-overs and birthday parties. Once again, meet the parents of talk to them on the phone inquiring what the evening's agenda is and if they will be constantly supervising the group.

4. If the situation looks bad, or if the peer group, parents or plans all seem questionable, simply do not approve of your child participating. Explain why and make a plan for the next gathering to be at your home.

Chores

Children should be required to participate in household chores. The assigned chores increase the children's sense of responsibility, self-worth and interaction with other family members. During this stage where industry is the mayor emotional challenge, participating and completing family chores increases the child's sense of contribution and competence.

To encourage children to compete family chore the following ideas are recommended.

1. Don't always give children the least desirable tasks to do. Taking out the garbage, scrubbing dirty pots and pans, or cleaning the cat's litter box could stifle anyone's participation. Let the children share in the more desirable chores.

1. Reward efforts to participation and completion of assigned chores. After the work is done, spend a little time with the child relaxing over a dish of ice cream.

2. Do chores as a scheduled family activity. Find an appropriate time that is convenient to all members. This may not always be possible, but try. Saturday mornings are not the only time that household chores can be done.

Family Home Practice Assignment

1. List a behavior that you have observed in your child in each of the four principal areas of development.

- Physical: _____
  _____
  _____
  _____
  _____

- Intellectual: _____
  _____
  _____
  _____
  _____

- Verbal: _____
  _____
  _____
  _____
  _____

- Social/Emotional: _____
  _____
  _____
  _____
  _____

2. List one long-term goal you have for your child.

3. Spend a minimum of 30 to 45 minutes every day playing, reading or practicing nurturing touch with your child(ren).

Chapter 10

Skills Strips

Goal: *To increase parents'*
awareness of children's
abilities.

Knowing what to expect of your children as they continue to grow will help them develop a positive self-concept and positive self-esteem. Children love to please their parents as a way of saying thanks for your hard work and as a way of feeling successful. When children know they please their parents, they aren't afraid to try new things and to work hard at completing tasks.

47

Skills Strips

Match the skill (behavior) with the correct age period. Circle the age you think children should be able to begin to perform the behaviors.

Behaviors	Age of Child				
	0 – 12 months	12 – 24 months	24 – 36 months	36 – 48 months	48– 60 months
1. Takes a few steps without support.	(A)	B	C	D	E
2. Repeats same syllable 2-3 times.	(A)	B	C	D	E
3. Builds tower of three blocks.	A	(B)	C	D	E
4. Says five different words.	A	(B)	C	D	E
5. Points to three body parts on self.	A	(B)	C	D	E
6. Uses pincer grasp to pick up object.	A	B	C	D	E
7. Imitates peek-a-boo.	(A)	B	C	D	E
8. Pulls off socks.	(A)	B	C	D	E
9. Holds and drinks from cup using 2 hands	(A)	B	C	D	E
10. Follows rules by imitating actions of other children.	A	(B)	C	D	E
11. Snaps or hooks clothing.	A	B	(C)	D	E
12. Pedals tricycle five feet.	A	B	(C)	D	E
13. Attempts to help parent with tasks by doing part of a chore (e.g. holds dustpan).	A	B	C	D	E
14. Walks backwards.	A	B	(C)	D	E
15. Will be attentive for five minutes while a story is read.	A	B	C	(D)	E
16. Sucks liquid from glass using a straw.	A	B	C	(D)	E
17. Imitates counting to three.	A	(B)	C	D	E
18. Puts on mittens.	A	B	C	D	(E)
19. Holds up fingers to tell age.	A	B	C	(D)	E
20. Uses word for bathroom need.	A	B	C	(D)	E
21. Stands on one foot for 4-8 seconds.	A	B	C	D	(E)
22. Uses words: sister, brother, grandmother.	A	B	C	(D)	E
23. Stays dry all night.	A	B	C	D	(E)
24. Takes turn with 8-9 other children.	A	B	C	D	(E)
25. Draws a man (Head, trunk, four limbs).	A	B	C	D	(E)
26. Engages in socially acceptable behavior in public.	A	B	C	D	(E)

Family Home Practice Assignment

1. Review your responses to the **Skill Strips**. Enhance your knowledge of child development by re-reading the chapters on **Ages and Stages** in the Parent Handbook.
2. Spend a minimum of 30 to 45 minutes each day playing, reading, and/or practicing nurturing touch with your child(ren).

Chapter 11

The Male &
Female Brain

Goal: ***To increase parents'***
knowledge of the differences
between male and female
brains.

The differences in the behavior between boys and girls can be attributed to the way the brain develops in males and females. Scientists are now discovering that the brain of a male is different from the brain of a female.

Male and Female Brain Structure

1. The human brain, both male and female, has 100 billion neurons.

2. Neurons connect to each other through neural pathways. The more activity that is associated with a certain part of the brain, the more neural connections are made and the stronger they get.

3. If certain parts of the brain are not used, neural pathways weaken and dry up. The brain is a "use it or lose it" organ.

4. Male and female brains produce hormones that support brain growth. The male hormone is called testosterone and the female hormone is called estrogen. Males and females have both testosterone and estrogen.

5. Between 3 to 6 months in the womb, the baby is being bombarded with different hormones. When there is more testosterone, certain areas of the neocortex grow and become connected. When the developing brain gets bombarded with estrogen and progesterone, certain other areas in the neocortex grow and connect.

6. If the child in the womb is a chromosomal male child (XY), the mother's hormonal system reads this as male and sends more testosterone. If the child is a chromosomal female (XX), the mother's hormonal system sends more female hormones.

7. In the womb, the child is being sexualized by the hormones it receives as either masculine or feminine.

8. The brain development of all babies, no matter what their sex, is stimulated by all hormones. All males have some estrogen; all females have some testosterone.

9. However, male babies get more testosterone and thus a more "male brain" develops while female babies get more estrogen and thus a more "female brain" develops.

10. The development of the male and female brain in the womb can be affected by the stress the mother experiences during pregnancy.

a. Physical abuse, illness and emotional distress can cause the mother's stress hormone (which is called cortisol) to cut off some of the normal surges of testosterone or estrogen.

b. It's possible for a boy to be born with a penis, testicles and other physiological male traits but with a female brain. The same is true for a girl. A female can have female physiological traits but have a male brain.

c. Some males report that they feel like a female trapped in a male's body. Some females feel like a male trapped in a female's body.

d. While males and females acquire new neural skills throughout life, the way the brain is set up during pregnancy does not change.

Notes and Comments:

50

MALE AND FEMALE BRAIN QUIZ

1. **Males would rather work on a project than talk.**
   True. More cortical areas in the male brain than in the female brain are devoted to the development of spatial skills like mechanical design, measurement and manipulation of physical objects.

2. **Males would prefer to read a book rather than play football or video games.**
   False. Since the male brain is devoting more cortical areas to spatials, less cortical areas are devoted to word use or production. In females, it's just the opposite.

3. **Males tend to talk less often and use fewer words than females.**
   True. The bundle of nerves that connects the right and left hemispheres of the brain is called the "corpus callosum." The corpus callosum is 24% smaller in males, resulting in males not connecting as many feelings or thoughts to words.

4. **Females act more impulsively than males.**
   False. The male brain secretes less serotonin than the female brain. Serotonin is the brain chemical that acts to calm us down.

5. **Males tend to be more aggressive than females.**
   True. This is due largely to lower levels of oxytocin in the male brain. Oxytocin is the brain chemical that helps us to be able to bond and demonstrate more empathy. The higher the level of oxytocin in the brain, the less aggressive the person is likely to be and more likely to link bonding and empathy in the verbal centers of the brain.

6. **Females and males bond differently.**
   True. Males rely more on "spatials" like playing basketball; females prefer to talk, relying more on "verbals." Bonding and attachment is influenced by hormones. Mothers have higher levels of oxytocin, which has been called "the nurturing hormone." When a woman is around small, helpless beings – babies, puppies, etc. there is a spike in this chemical. Fathers have much lower levels of oxytocin and therefore must bond and attach in different ways – socially, emotionally and psychologically.

7. **Males tend to be more patient than females.**
   False. Men take action first, talk second. Women are just the opposite. Lower levels of serotonin and oxytocin in the male brain are responsible for this trait. The male brain responds more quickly to obvious signals in action. Men are less inclined to stop, be patient, listen and communicate emotions verbally.

8. **Males have a stronger sex drive than females.**
   True. Men have a hormonal system that is dominated by testosterone. Testosterone is the sex and aggression hormone. Males have up to 20 times more testosterone than women.

9. **Males tend to zone out more than females.**
   True. Women's brains are constantly working. Whereas the male brain zones out and takes mental naps. Research shows that there is 15% more blood flow in the female brain than in the male brain.

10. **Males tend to solve problems by talking. Females tend to solve problems with action.**
    False. Males and females respond differently to problem situations. It's due to the way their brains operate. Males have "action oriented" empathy. Men are doers; they like to solve problems with action. Females express more of "feelings oriented" empathy. Women like to process feelings first, then work on solving problems.

Taken from "What Could He Be Thinking?" by Michael Gurian, St. Martin's Press, NY 2003.

Chapter 12

Developing Empathy:

Teaching Children to Care

Goal: *To increase children's ability to care.*

Empathy is the ability for one person to perceive the emotions, needs and desires of another person. It is the ability of one person to "walk in the shoes" of another person and feel what that is like. As it relates to nurturing parenting, *empathy is the ability of parents to perceive the emotions, needs and desires of their children, and to be able to respond in a nurturing way, keeping the positive welfare of the child in focus.*

Empathy comes from the Greek word "empatheia" which means, "feeling into." When parents are "feeling into" their children, they are in sync with them. Parents are "in tune" with how their young child is feeling. Since babies have not developed their verbal language to say how they are feeling, parental empathy is critical for the survival of the baby. As children grow up in empathic families, they learn empathy and, in turn, become sensitive to the needs and feelings of others. Empathy is clearly one of the greatest gifts parents can give their children.

How Does Empathy Develop?

Some scientists believe that empathy begins to develop when children are very young. When a one-year-old sees another young child crying, it is often the case that the child observing will begin to cry as well. From this physical imitation of distress, it is thought that children experience the same feeling.

Around the age of two, children become more aware that they are separate from others and will try to soothe a crying child. By two years of age, children begin to realize someone else's feelings differ from their own, and become aware that they are separate from others and will try to soothe a crying child. By two years of age, children begin to realize someone else's feelings differ from their own, and become more sensitive to cues of how another child may be feeling.

Late in childhood, advanced empathy emerges where children can understand distress in others beyond the immediate situation.

By the teenage years, teens can feel empathy about a social cause, and often demonstrate their concern in dress, demonstrations, rallies and community service.

Do All Children Develop Empathy Equally?

No two children are alike, therefore no two children develop empathy equally.

How Can Parents Help Their Children Develop Empathy?

There are several ways parents can help their children develop a sense of empathy:

1. **Use Nurturing Discipline Techniques.** Scientists know that the difference in empathy among children has a lot to do with the way they have been disciplined.

   Hitting, spanking, belittling, criticizing, are all roadblocks to developing empathy.

   Using nurturing, empathic ways to discipline presented in this handbook is a step in the right direction.

2. **Teach Children to Express Their Feelings.** Children have the right to express how they feel. What they need to learn are the proper ways to express those feelings. Parents who fail to show empathy to the range of emotions children express by telling them to quit crying, not to be angry, etc., teach children to avoid expressing, and perhaps even feeling certain emotions.

3. **Identify and Honor Your Children's Feelings.** When children express an emotion, identify and honor their feeling. An example:

   Mom: "Julia, you look so sad. Losing your bear is a sad thing."

   The result is Julia feels validated because her sadness was validated. Her mom honored the feeling and allowed Julia to accept and deal with her sadness.

53

4. **Model Empathy.** When parents model empathy they are teaching their children the caring way to react when someone else is distressed.

5. **Develop Family Morals.** Teach children that certain behaviors are morally right and wrong. Scientists now believe that the roots of morality are found in empathy, since empathizing with someone can prevent victimizing that person.

6. **Teach Children Responsibility.** As your baby develops into a toddler and a preschooler, help him understand the **Cause and Effect** concept of empathy.

   When children behave a certain way, their behavior sets off a response in someone else. A statement like: "If my father knew I was going to do this, he'd really be disappointed" is an empathic one because the child is concerned about how her dad will feel. Such a response to situations is much better than a child saying, "If my father knew I was going to do this, he'd kill me," or " .... I'd really get it," or such similar statements based on a pending decision or fear of threats.

   Two thoughts we have to share with you about the use of threats:

   #1 It's an absolute lousy way to raise children. In the beginning, children will probably respond to the threats, until they get enough of them and begin to resent being treated that way. Parents who act like bullies and threaten their children teach children how to act like bullies.

   #2 Threats don't mean much because very, very seldom are threats ever carried out.

   Nothing is as powerful as empathy in learning how to behave. The goal is to have children think ahead to what reaction could occur if they choose to perform a certain behavior.

7. **Observe Others.** When you're with your child in a store or watching TV, when appropriate, point out what you observe and ask your child to comment.

   Dad: "Look at that mom. She hit her son. Why do you suppose she did that? What do you think she's feeling? What's the child feeling?"

8. **Develop Family Rules.** No hitting, and no using hurting touch should be on every family's list of rules. Parents who care teach children to care.

9. **Teach Children to Care for Pets, Plants and Things.** Feeding pets, watering plants, treating toys and other objects with respect are excellent ways to teach empathy. Caring for other forms of life, and for objects, can also reduce the rivalry that can exist between siblings.

10. **Point Out Non-Verbal Cues.** Teach children to pay attention to the non-verbal cues of others. Since most communication is non-verbal, empathic children are good at interpreting how others feel.

11. **Teach Children to Share.** Sharing is one of the more important behaviors children learn to accomplish during childhood.
    It's difficult for children to share at an early age because they're struggling between hoarding everything and wanting to please their parents who want them to give their prized possessions up.

    As children develop their sense of trust in the world, they realize that giving something up is not forever, but temporary. After a short period of time, they'll get it back.
    A couple of things to keep in mind about sharing:

    1) Develop a family rule of asking and receiving permission to "borrow" an object that belongs to someone else.

    2) Not all things have to be shared. Some things owned by a child should remain out of the "shared" category. Examples might include favorite clothes and toys. Balancing sole possession with sharing is a good strategy to use.

54

12. **Do Unto Others ...** Treat your children and others, regardless of their age or abilities, the way you would like to be treated. Modeling empathy is a very powerful way to teach empathy to children.

Identifying and Honoring Your Child's Feelings

Here are some steps to help you identify and honor your child's feelings:

#1 Try to identify or label what your child is feeling. "Sammy, you're really afraid right now, aren't you?"

#2 Identify why your child is feeling scared. Your child will tell you why, if he knows why. Sometimes children have feelings and don't know why. Honoring their feelings is even more important when children don't know why they're feeling what they're feeling. If your child knows why, honor his reason. If he doesn't know, honor his confusion. In both instances, your child and his feelings are honored. "Why are you so scared? or "Do you know why you're feeling scared?"

#3 Honor your child's response. Your child may or may not know why he is feeling a particular way. In either case, honor the response he gives you. "Being afraid that there are monsters in the closet is very scary." "Feeling afraid and not knowing why doesn't help, does it?" <u>Don't say</u>, "There is nothing for you to be afraid of. There are no monsters. It's all in your imagination." or "Well, that's the dumbest thing I ever heard of - being afraid of monsters in your closet?"

#4 Brainstorm with the child what, if anything, needs to be done. Sometimes the situation may require that you and your child come up with possible actions that may help rememdy the situation. "Let's brainstorm what we can do to help you feel more safe."

Sometimes the situation doesn't need an action other than just comforting a child or sharing in their feelings: "Feeling frightened is not pleasant, is it?" or "We all need a hug and comforting sometimes."

Notes and Comments:

子供は "Why" と聞かれると答えにくいらしい。

子供の表情を見て…
例: "おこってる顔をしているけど…"

Step1. 子供は表現ができないので、
大人が (まちがっているかもしれないが)
子供の気持ちをはんだんする。

Step2. "どうしたの？"
"どのおもちゃが欲しいの？"
"おもちゃを探しているの？"
何が起きているかを子供と話しながら
状況をはあくする。

Step3. 子供の気持ちを尊重する。
"○○君が今・おもちゃを使ってるから、女とで
一緒に遊ぼうね"

Family Home Practice Assignment

1. List three ways your children demonstrate caring:

   a. _____

   _____

   b. _____

   _____

   c. _____

   _____

2. List three ways you demonstrate caring:

   a. _____

   _____

   b. _____

   _____

   c. _____

   _____

3. Identify three things you can to do encourage your child to develop empathy:

   a. _____

   _____

   b. _____

   _____

   c. _____

   _____

4. Spend a minimum of 30 ro 45 minutes each day playing, reading, and/or massaging your child(ren).

56

Chapter 13

Meeting Our Needs and the Needs of Our Children

Needs are the <u>SPICES</u> of Life

<u>S</u>ocial Needs
The need for friendship, for companionship.

<u>P</u>hysical Needs
The need for sleep, for food, for exercise.

<u>I</u>ntellectual Needs
The need for intellectual stimulation, for thinking new thoughts, for reading challenging books, for learning something new.

<u>C</u>reative Needs
The need to make something, to dance, to write a poem, to create something.

<u>E</u>motional Needs
The need for love, for praise, for feeling worthwhile.

<u>S</u>piritual Needs
The need to know that we are part of something bigger than ourselves and that we can increase our awareness of and sensitivity to it.

Goal: ***To increase parents' awareness of needs and behavior payoffs.***

57

Understanding Children's Needs

Needs are the basic elements of human life that are common to all people. Needs influence our behavior. People behave in order to get their needs met. The two are inseparable. If we are tired, we sleep; thirsty, we drink; lonely, we seek companionship; bored, we seek stimulation.

The basic needs that children need to live are no different than the basic needs of adults.

Young or old, capable or incapable, man or woman, boy or girl, all people have the same basic needs. What differs is the degree to which a person is needy and how dependent we are on others to get our needs met.

Dependency on Others

Many parents are on a developmental speedway trying to ensure children are self-sufficient as soon as possible. Toilet training, sleeping alone and through the night, and getting dressed are just some of the ways parents mistakenly believe they encourage a sense of independency in children.

Life is a set of stages going from dependency to independency. Natural development has to take its natural course.

Speeding it up only causes the child to speed through childhood with a life-long need to go back.

1. **Social.** The need for companionship is of importance during this period. In the first few years, parents are the major source of companionship.

   As children begin to make friends and play together, friends provide:

   - Companionship
   - Peer acceptance
   - Social involvement
   - Validation 確認

2. **Physical.** Basic to all life on the planet, but of particular interest to children. Some basic physical needs of young children include:

   - Eating proper foods, drinking proper liquids.
   - Sleeping 12 to 14 hours per day.
   - Being touched in warm, positive ways.

3. **Intellectual.** Rapid intellectual growth makes learning an exciting adventure. Intellectual growth is facilitated by:

   - Reading stories
   - Preschool
   - Exploring
   - Field trips
   - Hands-on activities

4. **Creativity.** A basic need is to express one's inner self; to be noticed; and to be unique. Some ways in which creative needs are expressed are in:

- Art
- Music
- Sports
- Dance
- Make-up
- Interests
- Dress and Style

5. **Emotional.** During the first five years of life, children undergo tremendous development. Basic emotional needs of children include:

- Consistency
- Trust
- Independence
- Love
- Autonomy 自主 (性)
- Security
- Fun
- Success
- Stability 安定

6. **Spiritual.** Spirituality is the need to belong andf be accepted. Some other ways spirituality can be accomplished are:

- Nature
- Synagogue ユダヤ教会
- Peer group
- Church
- Sports
- Mosque イスラム教
- Boy Scouts
- Girl Scouts

Empathy and Needs

Empathy is the ability of parents to be aware of the needs of children, and to construct an environment where children can get their needs met in a safe, fun, and nurturing way. When needs get met, children feel more fulfilled as people, and are generally easier to parent.

Needs also represent the milestones of development. As children grow older, the means by which they get their needs met change. Reading stories to children develops their own independent reading. Knowing the developmental needs of children, and having appropriate expectations are characteristics of empathic parenting.

Understanding Adult's Needs

Just like children, adults have the same six categories of needs that the body is programmed by mother nature to get satisfied.

1. **Social.** Adults need others in their lives. Without friends and family to help us share our responsibilities, life would be miserable and lonely.

2. **Physical.** Adults need to eat, drink, bathe, rest, exercise, sleep, breathe air, have shelter, and be touched by others to live. Sex is a physical need for the species to reproduce, but not a mandatory action for an individual.

3. **Intellectual.** Reading, discussions, listening to others, challenging opinions, beliefs and personal truths, brainstorming, problem solving, and figuring things out for ourselves all keep our brains growing and happy. Happy brains are thinking brains!

59

Sad brains are brains that lack stimulation, are full of old, useless ideas, just kind of sitting there in a rocking chair. A brain that's intellectually stimulated is a happy brain.

4. **Creativity.** Express yourself. Dress, talents, giftedness, style, culture, and appearance tell others who you are more than words. Creativity is the need to take a step outside the predictable and usual, the opportunity to act out just a little to explore options and to take the road less traveled. To stretch the imagination, and to occasionally take calculated risks are actions that expand one's horizons and give a different, perhaps more creative, outlook on life.

5. **Emotional.** Adults need to give and receive love, experience closeness and attachments, feel trust, acceptance, recognition, security, and intimacy.

6. **Spirituality.** To believe in something; to have membership; to belong; to have purpose - that's spirituality. A spiritual life is a meaningful life. Life without meaning gives hopelessness, lack of direction, a feeling of being lost in a crowd.

Stress and Burnout

The six needs mentioned form the basis of two important "E" words: Empathy and Energy. Empathy is the ability to be aware of the needs of others; energy is the ability to take some action. Energy is generated as a result of getting your own needs met. You may be empathically aware of the needs of others, but do not have the energy to do anything about it. Why? *You're burned out, overloaded, fried as a crispy critter and have only yourself to credit. Why did you do this to yourself? Good question.*

Most parents give first priority to their children; last priority to themselves. The result is stress, harshness and the desire to disappear and just have some time for yourself. It does not have to end up this way if you make a plan.

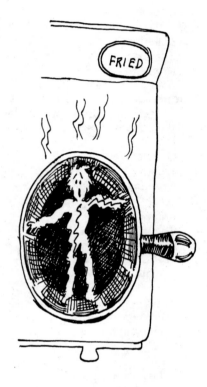

Family Home Practice Assignment

1. During the course of a week. discuss with your children the areas of needs presented. What did you learn?

    _____

    _____

2. Using the categories of needs to help children understand their behavior and the behavior of others. "Why do you suppose your baby brother is acting this way? What need do you think he's trying to get met?"

    _____

    _____

3. Use "needs" to describe your own behavior or desires:

    a. "Mommy needs some time alone now."

    _____

    _____

    b. "Daddy needs to concentrate on this project."

    _____

    _____

4. Take time to nurture yourself. What did you do?

    _____

    _____

5. Honor and respect your children's needs. Be helpful in assisting them to get their needs met appropriately.

    _____

    _____

6. Spend a minimum of 30-45 minutes each day playing, reading and/or massaging your child(ren).

"Getting My Needs Met" Exercise

Needs are daily demands, not periodically, occasionally or semi-annually. A day without your basic physical needs met can get one in a desperate straight. Actually, any and all categories of needs going unmet can generate a sense of desperation and people in desperate situations make desperate choices. One way to avoid having to make desperate choices as a way of life is to develop a plan to get your needs met.

Step 1: In the space provided, write down two ways you currently are getting your needs met in each of the six categories.

Step 2: Rate each need area on a value scale of 1 (low) to 5 (high). That is, how high or low is the value of each of the need categories.

Step 3: Rate each need area on a frequency scale of 1 (infrequent) to 5 (consistent). Your ratings should reflect how often you do something to get your needs met.

Step 4: When completed, review the need areas. Is your value rating higher or lower than your practice rating? Why the difference? Maybe you want to increase your activities in areas where practice is lower than value. Take the information generated from this exercise and make a plan.

Example:

Value: (low) 1 2 3 4 5 (high)

Practice: (infrequent) 1 2 3 4 5 (frequent)

"Getting My Needs Met"

1. **Social Needs:**

   a. _____

   b. _____

   Value: 1   2   3   4   5
   Practice: 1   2   3   4   5

2. **Physical Needs:**

   a. _____

   b. _____

   Value: 1   2   3   4   5
   Practice: 1   2   3   4   5

3. **Intellectual Needs:**

   a. _____

   b. _____

   Value: 1   2   3   4   5
   Practice: 1   2   3   4   5

4. **Creative Needs:**

   a. _____

   b. _____

   Value: 1   2   3   4   5
   Practice: 1   2   3   4   5

5. **Emotional Needs:**

   a. _____

   b. _____

   Value: 1   2   3   4   5
   Practice: 1   2   3   4   5

6. **Spiritual Needs:**

   a. _____

   b. _____

   Value: 1   2   3   4   5
   Practice: 1   2   3   4   5

62

Chapter 14

Recognizing and Understanding Our Feelings

Goal: *To enhance personal competence in managing feelings.*

"If I Only Had a Heart"

The Tin Man in the *Wizard of Oz* didn't have a heart and couldn't feel. He saw this as a limitation and sought out the wizard to get a heart. The wizard reminded him that hearts were only made to be broken and that he didn't know how lucky he was not to have one. Sounds like the wizard had his heart broken a few times, doesn't it? In the end, the Tin Man realized he always had the capacity to feel, he just never knew it. And maybe that's the lesson we all should learn: Everyone has feelings and it's fruitless to do anything other than learn how to recognize, manage and communicate feelings, and learn how to recognize the feelings of others.

"Your Face is Gonna Freeze That Way If You Keep Frowning!"

Most people have learned that there are two types of feelings: Good and Bad. We're not 100% certain, but we think defining feelings this way is the first step in messing everything up. In theory, there is no such thing as a bad feeling since all feelings are, in part, an expression of an experience. Feelings, expressed both verbally and non-verbally, have a purpose, and that purpose is to communicate a message. Simply, when we feel, we communicate. Additionally, the expression of feelings serves as a release of the energy that's associated with the feeling. Love wouldn't be love unless it generated the energy that propelled the person in love to act accordingly.

When we categorize feelings as good and bad, we also categorize the people who have them (including ourselves) as good or bad.

Rather than implying a feeling is good or bad, let's group them into the two categories of comfort and discomfort. In this way, it's the feeling we're labeling and not the people who have the feelings. Feelings of comfort include love, peace, joy, contentment, happiness, satisfaction, and all others that influence the person in a positive way. Feelings of discomfort, on the other hand, are feelings we try to resolve primarily due to the negative impact they often (not always) have. Feelings such as hate, envy, jealousy, anger, frustration, sadness and rejection generate an unsettledness. The goal is not to deny them, because you'll have them at different times during your life whether you choose to or not. Rather, the goal is to manage them so they, the feelings, do not overtake one's life.

How to Manage Feelings

There are three steps in the effective management of feelings:

1. **Awareness.** The first step in managing something is an awareness of what it is you're wanting to manage. The awareness phase has three components.

   - **The way your body responds to a feeling;** the certain name you give that feeling; being aware of your body is a key factor in being able to manage feelings.

   - **The name you give the feelings.** Different feelings influence us in different ways.

   - **Recognition of the situation or similar situations that generate specific feelings.** Such awareness can empower a person to avoid such situations, or realize that past similar situations have resulted in a specific feeling of discomfort.

2. **Acceptance.** The second step in managing feelings is a general acceptance that whatever you're feeling is OK, and that you're not a bad person for having such feelings. This step is more difficult than it seems. Rather than accepting a feeling, many people deny, pretend or mask the feeling.

3. **Communication.** Communication is the process of expressing feelings and thoughts. When it comes to expressing feelings, such communication can either be verbal or non-verbal. All feelings have energy which gives the feelings life. The key is how people use

their personal power to express the energy of their feelings. Three helpful rules in expressing energy are:

- Respect yourself – Don't hurt yourself.

- Respect Others – Don't hurt Others.

- Respect the Environment – Don't destroy property, animals or nature.

Sarcasm, ridicule, verbal abuse, hitting people and objects, throwing things, any kind of self-injurious behavior, are all unacceptable ways to use personal power to express the energy of the feelings. Finding acceptable ways to release the energy is the goal.

Hiding Your Feelings

When past experiences in our lives have been very painful, there is a tendency for many of us to not want to deal with the pain. We avoid dealing with the pain consciously or unconsciously. Since we do not want to, or are unable to deal with the pain, somehow we have to get rid of it. Some examples of painful experiences could be the death of a loved one, the breakup of a meaningful relationship, a bad investment of money, or some painful experience in childhood.

In these instances, and many others like them, we will either try to forget the experience altogether, or we will attempt to get rid of the painful feelings by stuffing them inside.

Neither works very well in the long run. The painful feelings do not go away; they are just out of sight.

As children, we learn not to feel pain, not to cry, and not to recognize our discomforts. We learn that boys don't cry, and little girls have to be little ladies who are pretty, neat, and clean. We learn very early in life not to deal with pain or other feelings of discomfort.

Letting Go of Past Pain

Think of experiences that you had in your childhood or are having now that have been, or are, very painful. Now think of the experience as a big spring, the kind you find in box springs and in cushioned chairs and couches. The natural position of a spring is to be fully extended.

To squash the spring, we have to apply a lot of pressure to keep the spring from being fully extended.

An unpleasant experience we've had that we are unwilling or unable to deal with acts as a giant spring that we have to squash by applying pressure to it. And since we don't ever want to feel the pain of the experience, we constantly have to keep applying pressure on the spring to keep it down. The moment we let up on the spring, it becomes fully extended, just like the painful feelings that come leaping into our conscious mind. When that happens, we relive the experience again.

Feeling Free

Our philosophy is to encourage you and your family to spend your energy using healthy strategies to express your feelings of discomfort, and not hide them.

Because some of the springs have become so big, using our energy to deal with the pain rather than to keep the spring down might seem really scary. The effort involved in feeling free and being able to nurture yourself and others may not be easy, but it is certainly worth it. The feeling of emotional freedom and growth is unlike any other feeling.

The risk to share yourself with others is the next step, and perhaps the biggest. All the other steps in comparison are smaller and easier. When family members take the steps together, the world you and your family live in now will never, ever be the same. The very act of letting go of some past pain is often all that is needed to feel better about yourself and others.

Furthermore, we think the statute of limitations should be applied to feelings of discomfort: after seven years they expire and can no longer hold you hostage to them.

Home Practice Assignment

1. Practice expressing feelings. Describe the event.

   _____

   _____

   _____

   _____

   _____

   _____

2. Come up with a plan to share your big hurts:

   _____

   _____

   _____

   _____

   _____

3. Identify three strategies to let off steam in a positive way.

   a. _____

   _____

   b. _____

   _____

   c. _____

   _____

4. Spend a minimum of 30-45 minutes each day playing, reading, and/or massaging your child(ren).

Feelings Exercise

1. One feeling that I have difficulty handling is:

   _____

   _____

   _____

   _____

   _____

2. When I have this feeling, I usually:

   _____

   _____

   _____

   _____

3. When I have this feeling, others around me usually:

   _____

   _____

   _____

   _____

4. One way I'd like to express this feeling is:

   _____

   _____

   _____

   _____

5. What prevents me from expressing this feeling the way I want to is:

   _____

   _____

   _____

   _____

Chapter 15

Helping Children Handle Their Feelings

Goal: *To help children learn how to handle their feelings.*

You Shouldn't Feel That Way!

- **Why are you crying? It didn't hurt that bad!**
- **Don't show me that angry face!**
- **There's no need for you to be so sad.**

How we prepare our children to handle their feelings will, in all likelihood, affect the quality of their life more than just about any other element of parenting. Feelings are that powerful. The worst thing we can do as parents is to ill prepare children for the tasks and challenges of life.

Children and Their Feelings

Learning how to handle feelings, particularly feelings of discomfort, is one of the great lessons of childhood, and one of the greatest challenges facing parents in their quest to raise healthy children.

Help children control their feelings and the world is theirs. Let them struggle in their ways to recognize, express and handle their feelings and victory will be theirs. So much of what can make the quality of life exceptional rests with the competence children have in handling their feelings.

能力

A personal sense of competence often equates to a personal sense of adequacy. Children who perceive themselves to be competent and who feel a sense of self-adequacy are simply easier children to parent and to be around. However, children who cannot control the intensity of their feelings, and who lack the competence to manage their behavior, generally take a lot more work to parent. Stress and burnout are often the outcomes when parenting high-intensity children.

EMOTIONAL COMPETENCE 能力

Emotional Competence is the ability for parents and children to be able to recognize and express their feelings in appropriate ways.

Ways to Build Emotional Competence

1. Let children know all feelings are okay. Children have to believe that all feelings are good and are quite useful in communicating. However, it's HOW the feelings are communicated that can either be okay or not okay.

2. Label the feeling you see or think you see.

   - "You look angry," or "proud," or "happy."

   This will give the child a feeling of being believed and respected.

3. **Do not dominate the conversation.** Let the child do the talking. Encourage sharing by looking interested in what your child is saying. Children can think better when someone is not advising, blaming or criticizing.

4. **Promote rationale behind feelings.** Ask the question, "Why."

   - "Why do you suppose he's feeling that way?"
   - "Why are you feeling so sad?"
   - "Why are people to mean sometimes?"

   It's a wonderful way to teach If - Then, the formula for logical cause and effect.

- "If children get hit, then they feel bad."
- "If you never share your toys, then your friends will never share theirs."

Understanding why others feel a certain way is another sure way of building empathy:

- "If a baby cries, then she needs something."

5. **Brainstorm with the child what, if anything, needs to be done.** Sometimes comforting a child is all that needs to be done, or simply just listening.

6. **When a child wants something, honor their desire.** If you are in the store and your child wants a CD, rather than saying, "No," tell him you wish you could get him the CD. "If I had the money, I would buy you that CD." Or, "That toy is fabulous! Show me how it works. Wow! I know you really like that toy and really want it. But lovey, we don't have the money to get you all the toys you want. Maybe this could be one of your birthday presents!"

   This can have an almost magical effect on a situation because you have joined the child, not forbidden him. Children feel you understand and appreciate their desires. This can be very restorative for many children. Once children realize that their feelings are honored, they are more open to listening to the logic why they cannot have what they want.

7. **Teach children how to express their emotional energy.** All feelings have energy that needs expression. Feeling energy ranges from mild to moderate to severe. Mild and moderate feeling energy can generally be released through talking. It's the high moderate and severe energy levels that get children into trouble. At this level, children often need a physical outlet for their energy. Brainstorm a list of physical things children can do to release their energy. Remember, do not condone actions that can hurt one's self, others or the environment.

8. **Praise, praise, praise.** When children are expressing their feelings appropriately, let them know you like what you hear. Remember, the behaviors you pay attention to are the behaviors that are being reinforced.

Home Practice Assignment

1. Practice honoring children's desires.

2. Help children express their feeling energy in positive ways.

3. Model appropriate ways to express feelings.

4. Spend a minimum of 30-45 minutes each day playing, reading, and/or massaging your child(ren).

Chapter 16

Spoiling Your Children

A child who acts "spoiled" is a boy or a girl who has learned to be disrespectful demanding, uncaring, and generally a pain to be around. Let's emphasize the point that the behavior is learned, and generally learned from parents who practice inconsistent parenting coupled with an inability to set proper limits. The lives of young children need a structured, warm and caring home so they can know what is expected of them. **"Spoiled" children are only behaving in a way they have learned.**

Parents worry a lot about spoiling children by giving them what they need or by paying attention to them, or by providing them with certain privileges. Parents who feed their baby on demand worry that their child will grow up being a demanding person. Parents who let their child crawl into their bed worry that the child will never get out. Parents fear that if they change their mind, their child will walk all over them. Parents fear if they negotiate and request cooperation rather than obedience, their child will be disrespectful. So many of these worries are not grounded on anything but old wives tales, myths and stories, many of which originated generations ago.

Goal: ***To increase parents' understanding of the practice of "spanking."***

71

Needy and Spoiled Children

All young children are needy. The goal of nurturing parenting is to promote growth and autonomy by helping children get their needs met. Children who don't live in homes where basic needs are met face serious consequences to their development.

Needy children generally feel insecure and unsure of their own abilities to get some of their needs met. Therefore, they cling to their parents or other adults, believing that only by staying close can they be assured their needs will get met.

Excessive neediness in children develops in one of two ways:

1. Needy children generally have had everything done for them by their parents, and therefore have not been encouraged to do things for themselves.

   In a sense, they have been treated as infants or "infantilized," that is, not allowed to grow in independence and autonomy.

2. Needy children can also be a product of a home where needs don't get met as a result of too many children in the family, children spaced too closely in age, single parenting, special needs that require added attention, non-empathic parents, or parents who are as needy as their young children.

Generally, spoiled children don't trust that their needs will be met, develop an infantile personality, whine, hoard their belongings, have difficulty sharing, and generally make life miserable for everyone around.

Children displaying such "spoiled behaviors" don't have positive feelings of self-worth; therefore they have difficulty understanding how their behavior makes life for others miserable.

For both the needy and the spoiled child, a systematic plan to develop their positive self-worth through success in being able to do things for themselves, and in learning how to make meaningful contributions, will go a long way in helping them develop more appropriate behavior.

How Do Children Become Spoiled?

Spoiling children is not an easy task. It takes a lot of time, effort, and attentiveness on the part of a parent to spoil a child. Spoiling a child requires a parent perform the following behaviors:

- Do everything for a child so he does nothing for himself.

- Anticipate a child's request so he never has to ask for anything.

- Spend all your waking hours together.

- Prohibit any type of short separation from the child; even having a babysitter.

- Only pick a child up when he cries.

- Be inconsistent in the limits and rules you set down so a child never knows what to expect.

- Blame the child for being demanding and demonstrating anger toward him.

Worries and Facts about Spoiling Children

Worry: I will spoil my child if I pick him up when he cries.

Fact: If the only time you hold your child is when he cries, the child soon learns he has to cry to be held. Picking him up only when he cries is a good way to spoil your child. Make sure you spend twice as much time holding your child when he's not crying. The child will at least learn he doesn't have to cry to be held.

Worry: Children who throw temper tantrums are spoiled.

Fact: Temper tantrums are a way young children express their frustration towards a situation or person. Young children are essentially very needy people; they want what they want now, not later. Setting reasonable limits helps children develop patience and delays in their need for gratification. Expect a few temper tantrums along the way and don't become too alarmed. Make sure you read the information on *Ignoring as a way of helping children learn other ways of expressing frustration.*

Worry: A spoiled child is one who has not been spanked.

Fact: Spanking a child never prevented one from becoming spoiled. The absence of reasonable limits and consequences for inappropriate behavior contributes to spoiling a child, not the absence of spanking. *Spanking is a type of hitting; hitting is a type of hurting touch; hurting touch is a type of abuse.* A nurturing parent uses other, more effective, means of discipline and punishment than hitting.

Worry: A young child is incapable of doing anything for himself.

Fact: Children can learn very early in life to participate in getting their own needs met. They can help in getting dressed, wiping their mouths after eating, feeding themselves, and brushing their teeth. Children enjoy doing things for themselves because they feel more powerful and more in control of their environment.

Worry: My child acts "spoiled." To cure him I have to become strict and harsh.

Fact: Strict and harsh responses will never cure anyone of anything - spoiled children included. Sometimes parents confuse setting limits with being harsh. All children need to have a set of limits that are consistent and founded on the morals and values of the family. Family rules are the obvious vehicle to accomplish setting limits. All of this can be accomplished with love and compassion. Being harsh and rigid only sets the stage for rejection, power struggles and more tantrums

73

Babies Can Never Be Spoiled

Many wives tales, stories and myths about parenting babies exist that confuse parents, especially first time parents. *Here is one truth that you can be absolutely certain about: You cannot spoil a baby.* Babies are needy, dependent children who require the constant care and concern of adults they are with. Holding them, feeding them, changing them, comforting them when they're upset, and playing with them to stimulate their growth are required of a parent. Performing these tasks with nurturing will help in the growth of independence and autonomy that will be evident as your child grows into a curious and playful toddler.

Encourage Healthy Child Behaviors

No child is ever born spoiled. Becoming spoiled is a learned behavior like being afraid of the dark or not liking to eat certain foods. Children learn to be spoiled from the people who serve as their primary caregivers.

- Help your child by helping yourself learn new, nurturing parenting attitudes and child rearing practices.

- Pay attention to the needs of your child without overdoing it.

- Promote independence by encouraging your child to do things for himself.

- Model for your child the proper way to handle disappointment, frustration, and sadness so he can act more appropriately.

Family Home Practice Assignment

1. Write down two or three myths about parenting that have been told to you that you know are not true:

   a. _____

   _____

   b. _____

   _____

   c. _____

   _____

2. How have these myths affected your parenting style?

   a. _____

   _____

   b. _____

   _____

   c. _____

   _____

3. Spend a minimum of 30-45 minutes each day playing, reading, and/or massaging your child(ren).

Notes and Comments:

74

Chapter 17

Building Self-Worth

尊敬

What is Self-Worth?

Our "self" is a composite of all the aspects of life that give us an identity. Our "self" is made up of our thoughts, feelings, name, culture, capabilities, competencies, family of origin, nationality, body image, appearance, parenting styles, relationships, and every other aspect of life, past and present, that makes us the unique person we are. Our self is our personality, our character, and our genes. **Our self is a picture puzzle made up of thousands of pieces all fitting together to make a picture.** Without all the pieces, the picture would be incomplete.

Our self-worth is the value we give that picture. That value can range from low to high and can vary during different times and circumstances of our life. One goal of life is to maintain a high self-worth; the fuel of life that drives our spirit to impact the world in a positive way.

Goal: **To promote the importance of maintaining a positive overall self-worth**

75

Children and Their Self-Worth

Self-worth is the overall value people have of themselves. A self-worth consists of what people think about themselves (self-concept) and how people feel about themselves (self-esteem). Three primary sources are responsible for strongly influencing self-worth:

Family: mother/father/brothers/sisters, etc.

School: other children, teachers, etc.

Community: friends, peer group, coaches, church, service organizations, etc.

The most significant of these is the family. The others gain in significance as the child grows older, with the peer group and school becoming leading influences of high or low self-worth.

Why is Maintaining a High Self-Worth Important:

1. People with a high self-worth generally treat themselves, others, and the environment with respect. People with a low self-worth generally treat others the same way.

2. Others generally like to be around people who like themselves. Being around others who are constantly degrading themselves is a major downer. 品位を下げる

3. Parents who value their own worth can more easily value the worth of their children. Children with a high self-worth do better in school, attract better friends, make better choices regarding alcohol and drug use, and lead more successful lives.

Self-Worth and Life's Experiences

During the 18 years of childhood, there are 157,776 hours of life spent primarily at home, school and with friends. A child's overall feeling of self-worth is developed from the way the child is treated by others during the process of growing up. The most significant of these are the early years when parents and other family members make the biggest impression and set the foundation for future growth.

It's the early stages in life when experiences primarily shape and mold the personality and behavior of a child.

When the experiences a child has are positive, the impact on the child's self-concept (the way he thinks about himself) and self-esteem (the way he feels about himself) is positive. The result is a child who behaves primarily in a positive way because it's the way he's been brought up. The opposite is also true.

When life's experiences have been negative, the impact on the child's self-concept and self-esteem is negative, resulting in a child's behavior being troublesome and quite possibly destructive and hurting. ***The goal is to create a home that maximizes the positive qualities of life and creates a solid foundation of positive self-worth.***

Our Self-Concept Plus Our Self-Esteem Equals Our Self-Worth

Self-concept, self-esteem and self-worth are terms that are often used interchangeably and incorrectly. It would be similar to using words like breakfast, lunch and supper interchangeably. Each has its own meaning.

76

Self-Concept = Thoughts
Self-Esteem = Feelings

Self-Concept is the way people **think** about themselves. A self-concept can be positive or negative. Some examples:

+ Positive Self-Concept
I'm a capable person.
I'm lovable.
I'm fun to be with.

- Negative Self-Concept
I'm incapable of doing anything right.
No one could love me.
I'm a bore.

Self-Esteem is the way people **feel** about themselves. Self-esteem can be high or low. Some examples:

High Self-Esteem
I deserve to be treated with respect.
I am worth something.
I accept compliments and can praise myself.

Low Self-Esteem
I deserve to be hit.
I'm worth nothing.
I reject compliments and dislike myself.

The way we **think** and **feel** about ourselves will determine our self-worth

Can We Improve Our Self-Worth?

Absolutely! We have to want to improve. Growth is a continuous process that keeps life exciting and worth living to our potential. Throughout this book, strategies are mentioned to help improve your self-worth. But, perhaps the most important first step is identifying the labels we have for ourselves.

The perpetrator and victim within us just love to make our lives miserable. Any time they can throw a monkey wrench into the works of life, they will.

One way they exert themselves is by the negative labels they have for who we are or for the things we do. A personal label is like a name that, over time, becomes an identity. When a negative label becomes an identity, it begins to eat away at our self-worth. Some examples of labels include:

Positive	Negative
Smart	Dumb
Able	Klutz
Focused	Scatter Brain
Friend	Jerk
Considerate	Absent-minded

It's not surprising that labels and self-worth go hand-in-hand. When people work on building their self-esteem and self-concept, the negative labels are quickly replaced by positive ones.

**The first step to change
is self-awareness.**

77

"Self-Labels Exercise"

1. Write down a negative label you have for yourself:

   Not confident

2. What do you do (or don't do) to get that label?

   Need to tell myself "You can do it"

3. What positive label would you like to have instead?

   Challengable

4. List three behaviors you can do to promote your new positive label:

   a. *think positive*

   b. _____

   c. _____

5. Every time you behave as your new label, give yourself a treat. Reinforcing your effort is an excellent way to change labels and grow.

Labeling Children

The image that children develop of themselves is, in large part, the result of parental perceptions. These perceptions are expressed in labels: names we give our children based on any element of their existence. These labels can be positive or negative. Some examples :

Positive	Negative
Cooperative	Uncooperative
Intelligent	Stupid
Active	Lazy

What's in a label?   An identity. It doesn't help that labels are used in school (gifted, learning disabled, etc.) and by a peer group (jock, geek, etc.) **In truth,** it's difficult for children to develop positive self-worth when it appears the world is ready to label them - with emphasis on the negative. *A good rule to follow is one that's centuries old: "If you can't say something nice about someone, don't say anything at all."*

"Changing Parents' Negtative Labels of Their Children"

1. Write down a negative label you have for your child.

   _____

2. What does the child do when she's being that label?

   _____

3. Write down the behavior you would like to see instead.

   _____

4. Give that desired behavior a name.

   _____

5. List three ways you can help your child perform the desired behavior:

   a. _____

   b. _____

   c. _____

6. Every time you see your child behaving in the desired way, tell your child how proud you are of their efforts. Throw in a a hug with the compliment.

7. Focus on the desired behavior. Consistent support is the answer to change that will last a lifetime.

Ten Ways to Improve a Child's Self-Worth

1. **Put children in situations where they can succeed at doing what you want them to do.** For instance, if a child is unsure of himself, give the child an opportunity to develop self-confidence by experiencing success, such as helping pick out fruits and vegetables, or pushing the shopping cart.

2. **Expect the child to succeed in a small, specific situation.** If you expect children to succeed all the time in all situations, you will be very disappointed. It is not a realistic goal.

3. **If your child does not succeed in a specific situation, problem solve and determine what is undermining the child's attempts at success.**

4. **Every time you see your child behaving in the desired way, praise him - and write it down.** Try to remember other times in the past when you have seen the desired behavior and then you can have a list or a "story" of successes. You can either read this to the child when the child is feeling down, or use it as a bedtime power story so the child can go to sleep with this new and successful picture in his mind.

5. **Tell someone else how the child is behaving, and make certain the child can hear you.** Call someone and recount the successes. If no one is home, talk to the dial tone. Make it realistic so the child believes you're sharing your pride.

6. **Act in a way you want your child to act, then praise yourself for acting that way.**

7. **Visualize your child as already being the new positive label, and then relate to the child with the new label as part of the child.**

8. **Show respect for the child's feelings and opinions even though you might not agree with them.** Honor your child's opinions and feelings by saying, "I can understand how you might feel this way." The child's feelings and opinions are a part of the child as much as your feelings and opinions are a part of you.

9. **Be careful to give children comments on their strengths as well as on their weaknesses.** Often we are so intent on helping children get rid of all their "bad" qualities that we neglect to comment on all the good ones we see. Keep track for a few days of the balance of your comments by dividing a sheet of paper into two columns; one labeled *Strengths* and the other labeled *Weaknesses*. Then put each comment in the appropriate side and see how you do. Try to have five to ten times the number of comments that focus on the *Strengths.*

10. **Be patient.** Change is an evolutionary process - not a revolutionary one. It takes time to change. Stay focused and above all, be consistent.

Family Home Practice Assignment

1. Complete the "Labels" exericises in this chapter.

2. Use positive labels.

3. Improve your children's self-worth.

4. Practicing nurturing touch with your children daily.

5. Spend a minimum of 30 to 45 minutes each day playing, reading, and/or practicing nurturing touch with your child(ren).

Notes and Comments: *(think about themselves)*

自己概念 +

Self-concept −

Experience + − ← Child → Behavior + −

Self-esteem + −

自尊心
うぬぼれ
(feel about themselves)

79

Copyright 2009   Family Development Resources, Inc.   www.nurturingparenting.com   1-800-688-5822

Chapter 18

Developing Personal Power in Children and Adults

Goal: *To develop a strong sense of personal power in children and adults.*

Personal power is the life force within everyone. It is the use of our inner energy to influence the quality of life for ourselves and for our children. Personal power is not our physical strength, but rather the drive to accomplish things, the will to love, the energy and commitment to create, to change, to build and to raise healthy, caring children.

As a parent, our goal is to develop our children's personal power and to teach them how to use it in healthy ways.

How Do We Acquire Personal Power?

To a certain degree, personal power is both innate and learned. Innate means we were born with personal power.

When a baby cries, he is using his personal power to let his parents know he is hungry, tired, wet or scared.

Since he can't talk yet, it is the only way he can let his parents know he needs something.

As the child grows older, he learns new ways to express his needs, wants, and desires. Exploring the environment, or getting something to drink on his own are some other examples of the ways a young child will use his personal power.

Another example of using personal power is getting the needs met to love and be loved. A young infant needs to feel secure and assured that mom and dad will love her and take care of her until she can begin to take care of herself.

Positive Use of Personal Power

The way children use their personal power has a lot to do with the way they feel and think about themselves. Children who have an overall positive self-worth behave in ways that treat themselves and others with respect.

When parents create a home with boundaries that allow healthy choices, safety and trust, children learn how to use their personal power in positive ways.

Negative Use of Personal Power

Not all children, however, use their personal power in a positive way. Some use their personal power in negative, hurtful ways. Hurting others, alcohol abuse, fighting, and constant oppositional behavior are some examples of the negative use of personal power.

People who commit such acts generally do not feel very good about themselves as boys or girls, men or women. Consequently, they don't feel good about others either. They use their personal power in ways that keep themselves and others feeling lousy.

Powerlessness

Still, others feel they don't have any personal power, that no matter what they do things will never get better, so why bother!

We call this feeling "learned powerlessness." Children and adults who are victims of child abuse and spouse abuse are good examples of people who have learned to be powerless.

Over a period of time, the messages they received and the violence they experienced tell them that they are inadequate and unable to do things for themselves.

As a result of learned powerlessness, some people remain in violent situations and relationships because they feel trapped and powerless to get out, or get out only to get involved in a similar situation.

Power Struggles Between Parents and Children

1. Power struggles are natural. It may not seem like it, but they are. Power struggles are a way of children gaining some autonomy in their life. They're trying to be their own person. Problems occur when parents or children start using their personal power in negative, destructive or hurtful ways.

2. Oppression is the seed of power struggles. History tells us over and over again you

cannot oppress people. Build walls around them, they'll knock them down. Enslave them, they'll run away or fight back. Try to take their opinions away, they'll think them secretly. Try to take their desires away, they'll dream them. Whether parents like it or not, children have personal power and the goal is to teach them to use it wisely and not to keep trying to oppress it.

3. Power struggles come in various frequencies (seldom to often) and degrees (differences of opinion to oppositional behavior). The most serious kind are the ones where parents and children are arguing all the time about everything.

Oppositional behavior is the worst kind of power struggle. It shows no empathy, no cooperation, and no perception that the other person's opinions have value. ***The most common type of power struggles are the "differences of opinions" that can be resolved through negotiation, compromise, and problem solving.***

What to wear, when to have a snack, how many stories to read; these are all easily negotiated power struggles. The beauty of these is in the lessons children received in finding ways to resolve problems and differences of opinion.

Empowerment and Children

Empowerment is a feeling of capability. To be empowered means to use your personal power in positive, healthy ways. Adults, however, often view empowered children with a cautious eye.

- Toddlers who are excited about life and want to explore the environment are labeled as "terrible." The "terrible two's" are adults; way of saying empowered children are a lot of work to manage. However, adults who explore and discover are called scientists.

- Children who express their opinion about issues in life are labeled as "opinionated" or "having a smart mouth." Adults who express their opinion are often referred to as "informed" or "having a moral conviction."

- Strong-willed toddlers are scorned by adults who try to break their will by demanding obedience to authority. However, adults with a strong will are thought of as leaders. Adults who act obedient are dismissed as having a weak character, gutless or followers.

Empowered Children and Mental Health

- Children need to be empowered early to withstand the peer pressures of drugs and sex in their teenage years. Saying "no" to unhealthy aspects of life takes personal power. The weak or powerless are easy prey.

82

- While any child can be victimized by others, children with a strong sense of personal power challenge, ask questions, examine the entire situation, make a personal assessment, and then decide.

- It takes a strong sense of personal power to cooperate, follow family rules, have a moral conviction, respect others, and succeed in life.

- It takes a strong sense of personal power to make healthy choices, control impulses, and seek help when needed.

To Develop Personal Power in Your Children

- Treat children with respect and dignity.

- Praise your child for being and doing.

- Give children opportunities for success.

- Encourage your children to take responsibility for their feelings.

- Provide your children with choices and consequences.

- Listen and talk to your children.

- Respect your child's body.

- Be nurturing and consistent in helping children learn appropriate behaviors.

Simply, children with a positive sense of personal power turn out to be leaders, are not easily swayed to act out of their moral beliefs, and believe that respecting and caring for themselves and others are important values to have. As you develop your sense of positive personal power, it will be easier to see the value in having your children develop their power. Personal power is our life force and energy. Teach children to use it for the betterment of humankind.

To Develop Personal Power in Yourself

- Take ownership of your feelings.

- Take responsibility for your own behavior.

- Make decisions to problems that will increase your sense of self-worth.

- Have a sense of spirituality (belonging).

- Accept praise from others.

- Follow through with commitments.

- Be aware of your own needs and feelings.

Notes and Comments:

Home Practice Assignment

1. Discuss with your family the concept of Personal Power.

2. Use the strategies presented in this chapter to build personal power in your children.

3. List the top five ways you use your personal power in positive ways and negative ways..

Positive Use of my Personal Power:

a. _____

b. _____

c. _____

d. _____

e. _____

Negative Use of my Personal Power:

a. _____

b. _____

c. _____

d. _____

e. _____

4. Spend a minimum of 30-45 minutes each day playing, reading, and/or massaging your child(ren).

Chapter 19

Understanding Discipline

Setting boundaries and limits for young children is one of the most important responsibilities of the nurturing parent. Setting boundaries and limits is called Discipline. **Discipline comes from the Latin word, dicipulus, which means "to teach and to guide."** Many parents think it means punishing children or being mean and harsh. It doesn't. Discipline is best defined as the morals, values, rules, guidelines, and standards for acceptable behavior that parents help establish for their children. Children need to learn right from wrong and which behaviors are acceptable in order to feel secure and to develop a sense of trust. If not, chaos, confusion and power struggles will be the order of the day.

To help children learn discipline, the techniques parents use will play in important role in whether children will learn to be cooperative, respectful and caring, or uncooperative, disrespectful and mean.

Goal: To increase parents' understanding of the concept of discipline.

To make establishing discipline for you and your child a positive experience, there are four very important points to remember:

1. The time you spend with your child has to be quality "time-in." For "time-out" and other techniques to work as effective forms of punishment, parents must have a positive, caring, fun relationship with their children. Quality time-in means:

- Holding and touching your child in gentle, positive ways.

- Playing with and reading to your child.

- Treating your child with care and respect.

- Showing that you care about your child and their world.

2. Parents must have expectations for their child that are developmentally appropriate. Expecting your toddler or pre- schooler to behave in a way that is not appropriate for their age will only result in feelings of failure, frustration and ineffective discipline. Equally inappropriate is expecting your baby to follow the rules set for your older children. A baby's brain is a work in progress and is not yet capable of understanding right from wrong.

3. For discipline to work, parents must be consistent yet flexible. Changing the rules or not enforcing the rules and values your family established will surely create a mess. Consistency is the best policy. But that doesn't mean parents can't be flexible. There are times when children can be allowed to stay up a little later, or when bath time can be skipped because it's getting late. Being flexible will keep you and your children from getting too stressed out.

4. Remember to take time to nurture your-self away from your children. Nurturing yourself will keep you fresh and excited to be with your children.

In establishing discipline, there are three important strategies that will be of help.

Behavior Management

Behavior Management is a general term used to describe techniques parents use to manage the behavior of children. When a parent is managing the behavior of their children, the parent is directly in control. Some examples of behavior management are:

- Danger-proofing a house so children can play safely;

- Feeding, dressing and diapering a child;

- Redirecting children from a dangerous place or activity to a safe one.

- Establishing family rules.

86

Babies need a lot of their behavior managed because of their developmental neediness. As babies turn to toddlers who grow into preschoolers, they can begin to manage many of their own behaviors.

While there is always some behavior management going on in parenting, the goal is to teach children to develop their independence and autonomy. This is where "behavior encouragement" comes in.

Behavior Encouragement

Behavior Encouragement is another general term used to help parents put the focus on encouraging children **to try their best, to cooperate, and to show respect and caring**. In Behavior Encouragement, quality time-in is the key. Some examples are:

- Praise for doing and praise for being
- Honoring children's desires
- Using gentle touch
- Encouraging children to cooperate
- Encouraging children to use their personal power

Behavior Encouragement techniques foster children's sense of personal power and autonomy.

Behavior Modification

Behavior Modification is yet another general term used to describe techniques designed to correct undesirable behaviors in toddlers and preschoolers. Some examples are:

- Time-out
- Being grounded
- Loss of a privilege

These techniques are used primarily as consequences for undesirable behaviors for children 2 years and older. **Babies are never punished for their actions. They are too young to purposefully misbehave.**

You can easily see that without a solid behavior management plan and an everyday behavior encouragement plan, behavior modification would need to be used all the time.

The constant use of punishment would be undesirable for any child and parent.

As you continue on in the Nurturing Program, you will learn techniques that will manage, encourage and modify children's behavior.

Family Home Practice Assignment

1. Discuss with your partner or others significant in raising your children the meaning of the term "discipline".

2. Identify the things you agree and disagree on.

3. List ways you currently discipline children.

4. Make a plan to "discipline as a team" so the children don't receive mixed messages.

5. Spend a minimum of 30-45 minutes each day playing, reading, and/or massaging your child)ren).

Chapter 20

Understanding Why Parents Spank Their Children

Goal: To understand common reasons why parents spank their children.

Hitting children as a parenting practice has been around as long as man has been recording history, and probably even before, which makes hitting children a prehistoric behavior. Yet, in spite of years or research documenting the limitations of hitting children as a parenting practice, spanking is still widely used today. So why does spanking remain so popular? Let's examine some reasons why.

Parents hit children . . .
because of personal history

Many people raise their children the way they were raised with one exception; those who recognize that the terrible things that happened to them as children are practices they don't want to repeat. Adults who were spanked as children tend to repeat those same patterns in raising their children.

Parents hit children . . .
to teach them right from wrong

Parents often hit their children because they want their children to learn right from wrong. Using the theory, "Where there's pain, there's gain," parents feel a "good spanking" will teach children not to misbehave.

The reality is that spanking communicates to children that they not only did something wrong, but they also are bad people.

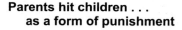

In addition, hitting never teaches children what to do or what is the right thing to do. Instead, it only teaches children what is not acceptable.

Parents hit children . . .
as a form of punishment

For many parents, hitting is the only way they know to punish children for misbehaving. If they don't use spanking, many parents are left with no form of punishment at all. Any mention of eliminating spanking as a form of punishment leaves parents with a basic fear that children will be allowed to do what they want and will be out of control.

Parents hit children . . .
as an "act of love"

Many parents feel that hitting their children is an act of "love" born out of deep concern for their child's well being. These parents tell their children how much they love them while they're hitting them.

Statements like, "If I didn't love you, I wouldn't be doing this;" "This hurts me more than it hurts you;" "One day you'll thank me for this;" or, "This is for your own good" send confusing messages.

If such interactions continue through childhood, children learn that people who love them are also   people who can hurt them

A common result is that many women choose husbands and boyfriends who show them love the same way as dear ol' Dad did.

Parents hit children . . .
to teach them respect

Parents demand that their children treat them with respect, yet use violence to enforce their demands. Any way you view it, violence is a most disrespectful practice and can never serve as a model of respect, but rather a model of fear and intimidation. What children learn instead is that violence is a way of getting others to do what you want them to do.

Parents hit children . . .
when they're angry

Parents who lose control are at higher risk for seriously hurting their children than parents who can control their anger. When anger turns to rage, the ability to stay in control is lost. *The key to controlling one's anger is not to let it get out of control by finding alternative means to release anger energy.* Physical exercise, talking, writing letters, walking or crying are just a few alternatives to letting off anger energy.

89

Parents hit children . . .
based on religious writings

"Spare the rod, spoil the child" is the single most misquoted and misunderstood phrase in literature. This phrase comes from Proverbs in the Bible, and has been interpreted by many people as meaning that the Bible sanctions violence toward children. Interpreted literally, the rod to many means a stick. Therefore, this proverb has been interpreted to mean that if a child's body is spared from being hit with a stick, not only will the child grow up spoiled, but also that the Bible has been disobeyed.

The actual verse that appears in the Bible is Proverbs 13:24: "He that spareth his rod, hateth his son; but he who loveth him, chasteneth him betimes." The notion of "spoiling a child" by sparing the rod was suggested later by 16th Century authors. Notable among them was Samuel Butler who, in 1663, wrote in Hudibras, "Love is a boy by poets styled; then spare the rod, and spoil the child."

The Hebrew translation of the Proverb offers several interpretations for the word "rod." Rod was, at times, interpreted as a scepter, a symbol of power, not of violence. *Rod also meant staff, a rod with a curved top used by shepherds to guide and lead sheep.* Some interpreted rod as a stick while others interpreted rod as a symbol for guidance. Many members of the clergy advocate guidance as an interpretation, believing that children need guidance, not violence.

Parents git children . . .
because it's a cultural practice

Many people believe that hitting children is a way for parents to express their cultural identity. Parents of different races and cultures all believe hitting is unique to their culture. Hitting is so widespread throughout society that hitting children is a societal practice rather than a cultural one.

Parents hit children
. . . to prepare them for the real world

Violence is widespread in today's world. We see it on TV, in movies, and in video games. We read about it in newspapers and magazines. We witness it in our neighborhoods and in our schools. Because violence is so common, many parents believe they need to prepare their children for the violence-filled "real world" by "toughening them up."

The reality is that the "real world" for a developing boy or girl is not outside their home, but within. What goes on within the home teaches and prepares children to handle the "outside world." Violence in the home is transmitted to the neighborhood. *The "real world" would become less violent if violence in the home stopped.*

Why is Spanking Detrimental to Children?

Children have the right to grow up in an environment free from violence, disrespect, and

90

hurt. They have the right to expect adults will treat them as valued human beings who deserve compassion, understanding and support. Parents would expect nothing less from their children; children should expect nothing less from their parents. The greatest limitations of spanking have to do with the impact on children's psychological development. The more frequent spankings occur, and the greater the severity of the spankings (beatings, thrashings), the greater the negative impact. Violence breeds violence. ***Children <u>learn</u> how to be violent, and a large part of the learning comes in the home.***

- Parents become people children fear and don't confide in. When fear takes over a parent-child relationship, there is a love-hate feeling that develops. Children love their parents for what they give them, but hate them for the price they have to pay for the closeness.

- Spankings out of love can grossly distort the definition of a close relationship. Once again, their experience of closeness is something that can bring about pain. Many people have difficulty getting close to others, and a large part of that difficulty can be retraced to the double message of "I love you and I can hurt you."

Simply stated: ***Do not hit your children and tell them you hit them because you love them.*** They will spend the rest of their lives trying to forget or work through that message.

Religion and the scriptures are all about love, kindness, service and goodness to our fellow beings. Spirituality is a basic need we all have to belong to something, to have strong beliefs in principles and values, and to have membership with a common group. Do you want your children to associate the goodness of spirituality with the use of a switch or belt?

In time of doubt, children need a belief in the goodness of life. Guidance, not violence, is the answer.

Parents' Personal Struggle to Change

It's difficult to break a habit - good or bad. Spanking a child is a parenting habit that seems like the right thing to do, even though we nay not necessarily feel better about what we did afterwards. So why the longevity of a habit no one really believes is a good thing to do? Let's examine.

"I Spank But I Don't Hit My Children"

Spanking is hitting a child on the buttocks with your hand or an object. Slapping is hitting a child on the face or hand or other body part with a hand or object. Beating is hitting a child all over with hands, fists or objects. Denial is pretending that something that is, isn't. ***Hitting a child, whether it's called a spanking, walloping, beating, thumping, whupping, smacking, or loving discipline, is still violence.*** Violence is violence and hitting a child is violence. The single biggest limitation to using this rationale: Children will learn to hit others and rationalize it's not really hitting.

"I Deserved to be Hit as a Child"

Really? Who told you that? Probably the people who most loved you - your parents. Do you think you would believe such nonsense if a stranger kept smacking you and told you the same thing? Bet not. It's difficult for adults to believe that, as children, they didn't deserve the spanking. After all, if we misbehaved, shouldn't we be punished? Punished, yes - hit, no. Big difference. Hitting is corporal punishment (body penalty). When you hit a body, you're telling the child ***they*** are bad, no good, unacceptable, inappropriate, etc.

When you punish other than by means of hitting, you're telling the child ***what they did*** is bad, not good, etc. See the difference? ***Corporal punishment means the child is unacceptable. Punishment other than hitting means the behavior (not the child) is unacceptable.***

The single biggest limitation to using this rationale: ***Children learn that being victimized is something they deserve in life.*** This philosophy destroys marriages and lives.

"I'm Doing This Because I Love You"

Hitting someone is a heck of a way to show them that you love them.

Forget sending flowers on Valentine's Day, send a slap-o-gram to your favorite valentine. I'm sure she'll think, "He loves me, he really loves me!" after getting slapped in the face by the slap-o-gram delivery person.

This business of hitting someone and telling them you love them is the craziest practice someone ever invented. Love is a basic need - to give it and receive it. Human beings need love to live. If you look up the word love in the

dictionary, you won't find hurt, pain, violence or cruelty in its definition. Love is respect, closeness, a spiritual intimacy, belonging, attachment - but it's NOT violence.

The greatest limitation to using this rationale: Your son or daughter might actually fall in love with someone who hurts them out of love, get married, have kids, and keep dancing to that song - in sheer misery.

Family Home Practice Assignment

1. Talk to your partner about the reasons why parents spank children.

2. Share the reasons why you were spanked. How did you feel then? Now?

3. If you spank your children, discuss why and what you hope to accomplish. Does spanking work?

4. If you spank. list four things you can do instead:

   a. _____

   b. _____

   c. _____

   d. _____

5. Spend a minimum of 30-45 minutes each day playing, reading, and/or massaging your child(ren).

Notes and Comments:

Chapter 21

Family Morals and Values

The basis for teaching children discipline is in identifying a set of family morals and family values.

Family Morals:
Beliefs of Right and Wrong

Family morals are the beliefs that family members have about right and wrong, and good and bad. Morals form the foundation of discipline. Discipline is the set of guidelines that teach children to make good choices, to cooperate, and to follow the family rules.

Some examples of family morals include:

- Treating others with kindness and respect.

- Not taking things that don't belong to you.

- Cooperating with parents by following family rules.

Without the moral basis of "right and wrong," as children get older they are likely to feel confused about boundaries, may not be able to make proper moral judgments, and may generally feel confused.

Goal: To help children develop strong morals and values.

93

Developing Values:
Beliefs That Have Worth

Family values are the moral guidelines that family members believe have worth. When a belief has worth, it has value. If "No hitting the family pet or other people" or "No fighting with each other" are morals parents are teaching their children, then parents have to practice what they preach. If not, parents create a double standard: It's **not** okay for siblings to hit each other or to hit the family pet, but it **is** okay for parents to hit.

The moral of treating the family pet and your brother and sister with respect will have little value, and hence will probably not be adopted. If a moral is to have worth, the entire family must practice it.

How Morals Are Developed

There are several sources that help young children develop their moral beliefs of right and wrong.

1. **Parents.** The primary source of moral development should be the parents.

2. **Extended Family.** Grandparents, aunts, uncles and other extended family members often play a significant role in the development of morals in the lives of children.

3. **Siblings.** Older brothers and sisters are a main source of moral development. Statements like, "You're gonna get in trouble if mom catches you," is a moral warning statement.

4. **School.** Children can spend the first 18 years of their lives being educated by other adults in day care, preschool, and 12 years of public schooling. Education strongly influences the development of children's morals.

5. **Peer Group.** The term "peer pressure" is the ultimate test on how well children stick to their morals.

6. **The Media.** You've heard the stories about the influence of the media in the lives of children. Parents need to monitor the content of what children are being exposed to on television, in movies, in video games, in music, and on the Internet.

7. **Church.** Religious education can play a major role in the development of children's morals. In many families, it does.

There is no doubt about it. Morals influence the food we eat, the lifestyle we live, and the parenting practices we use. Just about everything we do is somehow or another influenced by our beliefs.

Family Values

Babies begin to learn their morals by the way parents touch them, feed them, play with them, and care for them.

From the earliest moments of life right through their first five years, children are a work in progress.

And it is the way they're treated that will help shape their moral beliefs. Values are essentially the moral beliefs of right and wrong that have

94

worth; that mean something to children. Why is it that children who know right from wrong choose to do the wrong thing anyway? Statements like, "If I've told you once, I've told you a thousand times," or "If I catch you misbehaving, you're gonna get the belt," and other threats are probably a good bet why knowing right from wrong is not enough in doing right from wrong to have worth. For morals to work, they need to have value. Family value. All members of the family have to practice what's being preached. If not, the words don't mean anything. They lose their value.

Children Learn in Two Major Ways:

1. Direct experiences with their parents; and

2. By observing the way their parents behave and interact with each other.

If being caring and gentle to others is a family moral, but parents model disrespect and violence to each other and to their children, the moral has no value and being caring and gentle will not be a part of their children's lives.

The way children are taught, the way they are treated, and the overall quality of life in a family contribute significantly in the development of morals and values in children. As mentioned, morals and values form the basis of discipline. Research clearly indicates that the way parents choose to discipline their children is directly related to the level of caring children develop. Levels of caring or empathy in children are, in turn, directly related to how well children tend to go along with the discipline. Simply, children who are cared for tend to have stronger and healthier morals and values than children who

do not experience care as a consistent part of discipline.

weak morals

Family Home Practice Assignment

1. Gather your family members around the table or living room floor for a family meeting. Have some snacks and beverages. Mention to them the purpose of the meeting is to talk about family morals and values.

2. Share with your family information about morals presented in the Parent Handbook. Go around and ask each member of your family to share a couple of morals (rights and wrongs) they have. If the family is stuck, present topics like getting along, telling the truth, communicating and not fighting, etc. and ask for their views.

3. Tie in family values. Ask members which of their morals are highly valued. Come up with a list of five to seven family values and discuss why these values are important.

4. Spend a minimum of 30-45 minutes each day playing, reading, and/or massaging your child(ren).

Notes and Comments:

Chapter 22

Family Rules

Family rules are a set of Do's and Don'ts that serve as guidelines for carrying out family morals and family values and hence, creating the basis for discipline. Family rules are developed by all family members, apply to all family members, and are reviewed on a regular basis to determine how well the family is doing in following the rules.

- Family Rules involve everyone's participation. If grandma or grandpa play an active parenting role, they should also be involved.

- Family rules involve Do's and Don'ts.

- Do's let children know what is the appropriate behavior requested; Don'ts let children know what is not appropriate behavior.

- Family rules are designed to promote and reinforce desirable behaviors.

- Family rules help children learn appropriate behaviors through parental modeling.

- In family rules, everyone is treated fairly.

Goal: *To help children develop strong morals and values.*

The Purpose of Family Rules

The purpose of family rules is for parents and children to establish consistent guidelines that will help everyone know what is and what isn't expected of them. *Family rules encourage family members to take responsibility for their own behavior and to be contributing members of the family.* Family rules teach cooperation and make living together much more pleasant. Family rules also help ensure that everyone in the family has input into how the family operates and the standards of acceptable behavior. Family rules are for everyone in the family.

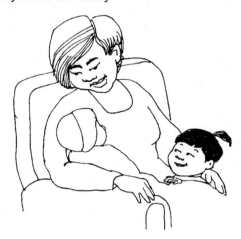

How to Establish Family Rules

There are eight easy steps to follow for establishing family rules:

1. **Get everyone to participate.** Have all family members sit around a table. Have young children sit on laps or be present even if they can't contribute in developing family rules.

2. **Share problem behaviors.** Encourage everyone to share family behaviors they feel are problems. Talk freely about issues the family has to work on. Avoid blaming statements and fault finding.

3. **Have a large sheet of paper (poster board) and a magic marker.** Draw a line down the center of the paper. On the top of one column write Do's; on the top of the other column write Don'ts.

4. **Brainstorm a list of rules.** Have children be active members in brainstorming a list of rules. The goal is for parents to have children come up with some of the rules they would like to see on the family list. Repeat this process until all issues are covered.

5. **Keep the rules simple and specific.** Be specific in wording your rules. Remember - for every "what NOT to do" there has to be a "what TO do." This way you're substituting what you want for what you don't want.

6. **Limit Family Rules to a maximum of five to seven.** Five to seven rules are plenty. Keeping a short list of rules will help children remember the rules and practice them. Too many rules are difficult to remember.

7. **Identify a consequence and reward for each rule.** For the rules to have meaning, a consequence must be associated with each rule. That is, when children choose to misbehave, a punishment must follow. *When children choose to behave by following the rules, a reward must follow.* Punishments and rewards teach the children that the rules have some meaning.

8. **Hold regular family meetings to review the rules.** Rules are not written in concrete. When a behavior is no longer a problem, have a rule dropping party. The rule has now become a family moral or value. When a new problem comes up, put it on the list of Do's and Don'ts.

Notes and Comments:

Family Home Practice Assignment

1. Meet as a family and make a list of rules. When completed, post the rules in an obvious place so parents and children can refer to them when a behavior needs to be performed. "Derek, I need you to follow our family rules and pick up your toys from the play room floor."

2. Recall a time during your childhood when you were held accountable to some rule and your brothers/sisters or parents were not.

   a. What was the rule? _____
   _____
   _____

   b. How did you feel? _____
   _____
   _____

   c. What did you do or say? _____
   _____
   _____

3. Spend a minimum of 30-45 minutes each day playing, reading, and/or massaging your child(ren).

Tentative List of Family Rules

Brainstorm a list of four or five possible family rules.

What to do	What not to do
1.	1.
2.	2.
3.	3.
4.	4.
5.	5.

Chapter 23

Rewards and Punishments

The discipline concepts we have learned so far state the importance of first setting up a list of family rules so parents can begin to guide and teach their young children appropriate behaviors. Also, identifying your family morals and teaching your children right from wrong by modeling those behaviors so children can see the "value" to the behaviors will help establish good strong family values. ***Morals, values and rules have to be established before using any of the following techniques.***

"If-Then" Philosophy

Discipline is based on an "If-Then" philosophy. This means: <u>If</u> your child performs an appropriate behavior, <u>then</u> a reward follows. <u>If</u> your child purposefully performs an inappropriate behavior, <u>then</u> a punishment follows.

Goal: To increase parents' knowledge and use of nurturing behavior management techniques.

What are Consequences?

A consequence is an action that follows behavior. There are two kinds of consequences: logical and natural. Logical consequences you plan, like sending a child to time-out or praising a child's appropriate behavior. Natural consequences happen all by themselves, like walking in the rain without an umbrella and getting wet.

Consequences allow children who are capable of knowing right from wrong the ability to take responsibility for their behavior.

Children will often choose to act a certain way based on the expected consequences. The type of consequence and the way it is administered will strongly influence whether the behavior will return. Positive conssequences, like rewards, work to reinforce appropriate behavior. Negative consequences, like punishments, work to eliminate inappropriate behavior.

What are Rewards?

A reward is a pleasant consequence for behaving in an appropriate or desirable way. The purpose of rewards is to reinforce good behavior. Rewards let children know how pleased parents are with their behavior. Rewards are necessary and important in helping children learn right from wrong. Rewards such as praise, nurturing touch and privileges tell children you appreciate their efforts.

What is Punishment?

A punishment is an unpleasant consequence for behaving in an inappropriate way. Punishment is a penalty for purposefully doing something inappropriate. The purpose of punishment is to decrease the likelihood that inappropriate behavior will occur again. It is not the purpose of punishment to hurt children.

Corporal punishment, like spanking, slapping, punching, etc., is an unpleasant consequence that physically hurts children, not their behavior. Punishment is a necessary part of discipline; helping children learn right from wrong, but hitting children's bodies with your hand or an object is never okay, and should never be practiced.

Other techniques such as time-out, loss of privilege, and being grounded are far more effective in helping children learn right from wrong.

When Should Discipline Begin?

Discipline, which means guiding and teaching, should begin right from birth.

Hoe Do Parents Discipline Babies?

Parents teach and guide their babies through the following:

- Playing with your baby
- Reading to your baby
- Singing to your baby
- Talking to your baby
- Modeling a healthy lifestyle
- Massaging and touching your baby
- Establishing nurturing parenting routines described in this handbook

101

- Having appropriate expectations for your child
- Praising baby for all the wonderful things she did.

However, it is appropriate for parents to use words like "gentle" when baby is touching brother or "owee" when baby pulls daddy's beard. By gently holding the hand and saying, "gentle, little one," parents are teaching baby the value of gentle touch.

When Should Rewards Begin?

Rewards form the basis of positive discipline. Two of the most powerful rewards a parent can use are praise and gentle touch. These rewards can begin at birth. Touching a baby in a gentle way is important for the baby's brain to develop and for the parent-child bond to grow strong. Children love being touched in a gentle way.

Praising a baby for all the wonderful things baby does and for the beautiful person baby is also can begin at birth or before when mom is pregnant and is carrying baby.

As babies grow into toddlers and preschoolers, praise and touch can continue as rewards along with special privileges and objects such as toys or stars and stickers.

Children love to be recognized and receive recognition. It molds their feelings of self-worth.

Should Babies be Punished?

Punishments are administered by parents to help children learn the difference between appropriate and inappropriate behaviors. **Babies should never be punished because their brains are not capable of understanding right from wrong**, and the purpose of punishment is to teach children right from wrong. Never punish babies.

Around 7 months of age, most children begin to make associations between two activities. For example, running water means tubby time is near; sitting in the high chair means yummy mushed peas or carrots are coming.

If parents punish babies, they will become frightened and anxious. They will associate this fear with their parent - not with what they did or didn't do.

Also, the stress and fear the babies feel when punished cause their brains to release stress hormones. These stress hormones affect the baby's brain in negative ways which can lead to sleep problems, hyperactivity, impulsivity and excessive crying.

Research has also found that babies who are punished excessively have 20% to 30% smaller areas of their brains that are responsible for controlling emotions.

Never Punish Babies!
Never Hit Babies!
Never Yell at Babies!
Never Shake Babies!

102

When Should Punishments Begin?

The goal of punishment is to help children replace inappropriate behavior with appropriate behavior. Punishments will only work under the following conditions:

1. If children can understand that what they did was inappropriate;

2. That this inappropriate behavior was a choice and not exploratory;

3. That the great majority of the time parents spend with their children is positive;

4. That the primary purpose is to teach what TO do rather than teach what NOT to do;

5. And that children are always treated with respect.

If these conditions are present, punishments in the form of time-out, or loss of privilege or being grounded can begin around 2 ½ years of age.

Techniques for Rewarding Children's Behavior

Rewards are very powerful in motivating children. Use the following types of rewards to help children feel good about themselves and learn appropriate behaviors.

1. **Praise**. Praise is the single most powerful reward a child, or anyone can receive. Praise will be discussed in greater detail in Chapter 24.

2. **Nurturing Touch**. There are three types of touch: hurting, scary and nurturing. Each of us has a personal touch history which includes all three types of touch. *Gentle hugs, back rubs, soft strokes of a child's back with gentle rocking, are all nice, positive types of nurturing touch.* Everyone wants recognition. Nurturing touch is a nice way to let children know you value them. Use nurturing touch with praise. Together they make a powerful combination.

3. **Privileges**. Privileges serve as excellent rewards for children. A privilege can be extra TV time, getting to stay up past curfew, getting a few extra stories read at night, or other behaviors your children enjoy. Privileges should never include basic needs the child has such as fun times as a family, security, love or trust.

4. **Allowance**. Teens, like adults, like to receive money. Money gives teens power to meet some of their own needs and teaches responsibility. Paying teens an allowance for completing family chores is a nice way to reward for "doing."

5. **Objects**. Some parents like to reward their children with various objects in addition to praise and touch. Objects can include almost anything that ranges from stickers to assorted toys. Find out what your child likes and occasionally reward him or her with an object.

Techniques for Punishing Cihldren's Behavior

There are five types of punishment that are appropriate for children ages 2 ½ and older.

1. **Loss of Privilege.** A privilege is a right granted by the parent. Privileges can be watching TV, playing with a certain toy in the house, etc. If a child misuses an object or misuses the privilege, they lose it for awhile. Take away a toy or a privilege only when the child misuses it (thrown, broken, etc.)

2. **Being Grounded.** When a child repeatedly leaves the yard without permission, an appropriate punishment is being grounded to the yard or house. The child must know it wasn't appropriate to leave the yard. If the child does not understand the behavior was inappropriate, grounding will not work as a punishment. Again, it's important for children to know what is expected of them.

3. **Parental Disappointment.** *Parental disappointment is a simple statement which expresses the disappointment a parent has in a behavior the child has chosen to perform.* The intent is to build some caring and an awareness in the child of the parent's disappointment. An example of the use of parental disappointment is: "Son, I want you to know how disappointed I am that you chose to hit your brother (or whatever the misdeed). I'm sure the next time you're upset, you won't hit your brother and you will tell him not to take away your toys." If the behavior is recurring, a parent may then also tell the child he either loses a privilege or has to take a time-out.

With school aged children, an awareness of appropriate and inappropriate behavior can be fostered through feelings of guilt and empathy. We try expecting you to act responsibly, but I see that at times you choose to act irresponsibly." Empathy, n awareness of the feelings of others, is a desirable trait you will want to foster in your children long term. Guilt, when used within acceptable limits, is an internalized behavior control that we all need. We need to use caution and not instill in our older children high degrees of guilt. Too much guilt will eventually be outwardly expressed as anger.

4. **Restitution.** Restitution means that there is a "payback" or logical consequence for a specific misbehavior. The goal of restitution is to make good of a wrong. If children choose to color on the walls, the payback is to clean the wall. If stealing is the problem, the restitution is to pay back the stolen money.

In the case of school aged children, if they are receiving a monthly or weekly allowance, then money can be used as a form of restitution. For example, if they leave their bicycle in the driveway, or when they destroy something on purpose, or when they throw and break something, they can be charged money from their allowance. If the behavior is repeated, a greater percentage of the allowance can be used as payment.

5. **Time-Out.** Time-out is a temporary isolation of the child from others because they chose to act inappropriately. It is a technique that lets children know that when they choose to behave inappropriately, they have to be by themselves for a while sitting quietly. Time out will be discussed in greater detail in Chapter 26.

The Dozen Rules of Discipline:

Rule #1: Help children learn appropriate behavior by involving them in direct experiences which will teach then the desired behaviors, and have them observe you behaving in the manner you want them to behave.

Rule #2: Behaviors need consequences following them to help children learn right from wrong. Consequences following desirable behavior are called Rewards. Consequences following undesirable behaviors are called Penalties or Punishments.

Rule #3: What you pay attention to is what you get more of. One of the important goals of parenting is to catch your children behaving.

Rule #4: Punishments are used to help children change inappropriate behavior, and only work effectively when used in conjunction with rewards to reinforce appropriate behavior.

Rule #5: Punishments are never used to abuse, injure or cause harm, or the threat of harm to children.

Rule #6: Time-out will only work when time-in is quality time. If time-in is not quality time, the child is already emotionally in time-out.

Rule #7: Time-out should be used sparingly and for teaching young children. Other forms of punishment are more appropriate for older pre-teens and adolescents.

Rule #8: The punishment must fit the crime. It must also be reasonable, respectful, and related.

Rule #9: The goal of punishment is to be meaningful and quick. Punishments of duration provide little motivation to do better.

Rule #10: If you misuse it or abuse it, you lose it for a while, then get another chance to use it. One of the goals of discipline is to teach appropriate behavior. If children never get another chance, how are they going to learn?

Rule #11: If you break it, you pay for it. If you mess it up, you clean it up. Restitution is an excellent way to teach children there are consequences for their inappropriate behavior.

Rule #12: Babies should NEVER be punished. They are too young to understand the "If-Then" rule of consequences.

Family Home Practice Assignment

1. Discuss rewards and punishments as a family

2. Practice using the techniques for rewarding behavior. Describe the outcome.

   a. Praise: _____

   _____

   _____

   b. Nurturing Touch: _____

   _____

   _____

   c. Privilieges: _____

   _____

   _____

   d. Objects: _____

   _____

   _____

3. If appropriate, practice using one of the techniques for punishing behavior.

   e. Which one did you use and why? _____

   _____

   _____

   f. What was the outcome? _____

   _____

   _____

4. Spend a minimum of 30-45 minutes each day playing, reading, and/or massaging your child(ren).

Chapter 24

Praising Children and Their Behavior

Praise can be a compliment, gesture, facial expression, or form of gentle touch like hugs or high-fives that promote feelings of self pride, worth and accomplishment in others. As a parenting practice, praise gives children positive feedback to increase their feelings of competence and confidence in themselves and their behavior.

Praise is the parenting practice of letting children know they have value as people, and their efforts in behaving and following the rules are appreciated.

Goal: *To increase the self-worth of children through positive recognition.*

Why is Praising Children and Their Behavior Important?

- When children receive praise they learn that who they are, and the things they do, are pleasing to parents.

- Children who are praised for their behavior, or for their personal qualities, develop a personal sense of self-worth.

- Praise is like fuel that powers the positive self-esteem of children. Children who sincerely believe they have worth treat themselves and others in positive ways.

- Years of research have indicated that children with positive self-worth get better grades, are more popular in school, do not get discouraged easily, and generally live more productive lives.

Roadblocks to Using Praise

- There is a popular myth that if children are praised they will become conceited, a feeling that they are better than others. The fact is, children who are praised develop a strong sense of self and do not need to put themselves above others to feel good about themselves. They already do.

- Some parents just expect their children to do what they're told to do without having to praise them. The fact is, nobody, adult or child, can behave in appropriate ways without some form of recognition.

- Many adults have not had the experience of receiving praise as children for them to practice the skill as parents.

- Adults who have difficulty accepting compliments from others will clearly feel very uncomfortable in offering praise to their children.

There are Two Types of Praise:

Praise for BEING

Praise for DOING

There are two ways to use praise as a parenting practice. One way is called **"Praise for Being,"** the other way is called, **"Praise for Doing."**

Praise for Being is the highest form of praise a child, or anyone else for that matter, can receive. It tells children that just because they are your son or daughter they have value and worth. *Praise for Being lets children know you value them for just who they are.* It is unconditional and given freely at any time. Some Praise for Being statements are:

- "I really love you!"
- "You're a beautiful person."
- "What a special child you are."
- "I am so happy you are my son."
- "You're a wonderful daughter."

When you praise children for Being, they don't have to do anything to earn it. *Praise for Being is a powerful parenting practice for building a positive sense of self-worth in children.*

Praise for Being praises a child for whom he or she is.

Praise for Doing lets children know you appreciate and value their efforts and behaviors. Children love to please their parents. When they hear **Praise for Doing** something, they know they've pleased mom and dad. Praising a child's behavior can be for something they tried and completed, or tried but didn't quite succeed at or finish. As parents, if you acknowledge your children's efforts, they are more likely to try again.

Some **Praise for Doing** statements are:

- "I'm really pleased to see you try so hard."
- "You buttoned all your buttons. Good for you!"
- "I'm so proud of the way you cooperated."
- "You're really doing well in school."

Using Praise Incorrectly

Many parents unknowingly use praise incorrectly by using **Praise for Being** and **Praise for Doing** together. Such statements are:

- "What a nice job cleaning your room. You really are a good girl."
- "Daddy really loves you for cooperating with me."

Such statements tell children you only love or appreciate them when they do something that pleases you. It's known as "conditional love" - love that has to be earned.

Children quickly learn to resent such love because they know if they don't "do the right thing," mommy and daddy won't love them.

Promoting Self-Praise in Children

Self-praise is a way children learn the habit of praising themselves and boosting up their self-image. To help a child learn self-praise, parents need to describe how good the act must have made the child feel. "Tracie, I bet you feel really proud of the nice job you did in cleaning your room." Imagine yourself in the child's shoes, and describe the feeling. By promoting self-praise, children learn to be their own best friend and develop self-confidence.

To encourage children to use self-praise, parents should model the behavior for them. Praise yourself in the presence of your children whenever you do something well, or whenever you feel good about yourself. Modeling self-praise is an effective teaching procedure because children learn best by imitation.

Being Conceited

Some parents worry about their children growing up feeling conceited because they received praise for the people they are or the things they do. Conceit is different from self-worth. When children feel conceited, they are usually sending the message that, "I'm better than you." Contrary to belief, it's children who don't have a positive self-image that wind up feeling conceited.

In this sense, conceit is their effort to elevate their self-worth at the expense of others.

How to Use Praise

To praise appropriately, follow the steps listed below:

1. **Focus your attention on the child and the situation** - praise deserves your undivided attention.

2. **Move close to the child** - praise feels good by someone close to you.

3. **Make eye contact with the child on the child's level.** For instance, stoop down to make eye contact with a five-year-old - this makes it all the more special.

4. **Gently touch the child** - touch is a positive form of communication.

5. **Look pleasant** - everyone likes to see a happy face.

6. **Praise your child** for being or for doing.

7. **Offer a hug** to "seal" the nice words.

Accepting Praise as an Adult

Praise is fuel for our positive self-worth. When someone offers us a compliment, they're actually fueling up our self-worth. Self-worth is the value we have for our self: our ideas, accomplishments, successes, as well as our appearance, personality and character. When others praise any of these qualities, they are doing us a big favor - they are recognizing us in a positive way.

Why is Accepting Praise Important?

1. It sends a message to others that we are worthy of their recognition and deserving of it.

2. When we accept a compliment, we are building our positive self-worth. Parents with a positive sense of self-worth can, in turn, help build the positive sense of self-worth in children.

3. As models, parents show their children that accepting praise is the right thing to do.

4. Everyone needs recognition. Accepting praise is a positive form of recognition.

5. When we accept a compliment, we're more likely to send one.

Rejecting a Gift

When we were young, most of us were taught some very basic elements of courtesy: When you want something, you ask nicely with a "please!" When you're given a gift, how many times did you hear from some grown-up, "Now what do you say?" and we retort with a "thank you." Well, whatever happened to that lesson? For a lot of adults, they've simply forgotten how to say thank you when they receive the gift of recognition. Someone offers us a compliment, we hide and blush and try to become the invisible man or woman – anything but a compliment!

How NOT to Respond

Compliment: "My, don't you look nice today!"

Response: "Well, I feel miserable."

Compliment: "Nice report, John."

Response: "Well, if I'd had more time, I could've done better."

What's the matter with this picture? Clearly, we wouldn't say such dumb things if someone gave us a bonus.

Compliment: "Larry, you've been working hard. Here's fifty dollars. You and your wife go have dinner on the company."

Response: "What? A measly fifty dollars? What kind of junk food do you want us to eat?"

If that was actually Larry's response, you can bet it would be the last fifty dollars he'd ever get from his boss. Which is what happens to others who offer us a fifty dollar compliment and we reject it. Bet on it, you will quit getting any compliments at all. And, when that happens, the fuel supply to your self-worth will be drastically cut short. In essence, you'll have to ration your self-worth because of the shortage of fuel you created.

How to Accept a Compliment

1. Look pleasant. Let the person sending the compliment see you enjoy being recognized.

2. Say "Thank you." Do not reject or send the compliment back ("Well, you look nice/work hard, too?") Be gracious and accept the gift.

3. Use gentle touch. A touch on the arm or a hand shake conveys your true appreciation.

Notes and Comments:

Family Home Practice Assignment

1. Practice praising your child(ren) two times a day for being and two times a day for doing.

2. Praise yourself once each day for being and doing.

3. Keep count of the number of times people offered you a compliment in one day. How did you respond?

_____

_____

_____

_____

_____

4. Keep count of the number of times you praised yourself in one week. Which one do you remember the most?

_____

_____

_____

_____

_____

5. Spend a minimum of 30-45 minutes each day playing, reading, and/or massaging your child(ren).

110

Chapter 25

Touching My Children and My Touch History

Goal: *Increase parent's understanding of the importance of positive touch.*

Touch is a very important part of the nurturing parent-child relationship. For newborns, touch is basically how babies begin to communicate. Many professionals believe that touch is our first sensory experience coming into this world, and our last sensory experience leaving this world. Without a doubt, our experiences with touch throughout our life time significantly influence our perceptions of the world as a safe or dangerous place.

The earliest research regarding the importance of touch was done in the 1940's. Studies conducted during this time found that children who were placed in hospitals and deprived of physical contact with their mothers developed profound depression and a lack of appetite. More recent research studies have found that babies deprived of touch showed a decrease in growth. Only when provided with human touch did these babies begin to grow.

111

Benefits of Touch

There are many benefits to touch:

- **Promotes Brain Development.** Newborns who receive extra touch have enhanced brain development.

- **Models Positive Communication.** In many ways the way we touch our children is our first communication with them.

- **Increases Bonding.** Touch is an important aspect in creating a strong parent-child bond.

- **Improves Digestion.** Touch makes babies digestive system work more efficiently.

- **Improves Behavior.** Babies who are touched and held frequently sleep better at night, fuss less during the day, and relate better to caregivers.

- **Reduces Stress.** Systematic touch decreases stress by decreasing the levels of the hormone cortisol which is elevated during periods of stress.

- **Promotes Development.** Babies who regularly receive gentle touch show increase weight gain and improved body tone.

- **Decreases Depression.** Systematic massage increases dopamine and serotonin levels which elevates moods and thereby decreasing depression.

Our Touch History

Everyone has a touch history. Our history reflects the experiences we have related to touch that are carried as cellular memories. Memories contain the events along with the emotions that the events invoked. Some people feel very comfortable with giving and receiving touch, while others shy away from touch. For some, the thought of giving or receiving touch carries real fear.

Touch can be classified into three categories: Nurturing, Hurting and Scary.

Nurturing Touch represents all the good and gentle touches we receive like massages, hugs, hand shakes, and pats.

Hurting Touch represents all the touches that are painful. Spankings, beatings, cuts, scrapes and fights are examples of hurting touch.

Scary Touch represents all the unwanted sexual touch, the threats of hurting touch, as well as the anxiety we experience as kids going to the dentist and medical doctors.

Complete the following statements reflecting on the different types of touch you received in your life.

My Touch History Questionnaire

1. In my lifetime, the percentage of touch I received in the following areas are:

    a. Gentle Touch _____ %

    b. Hurting Touch _____ %

    c. Scary Touch _____ %

2. Examples of **Gentle Touch** I have received are:

    _____

    _____

3. Examples of **Hurting Touch** I have received are:

    _____

    _____

4. Examples of **Scary Touch** I have received are

    _____

    _____

5. The percentage of touch I have given to others in my lifetime is:

112

a. Gentla Touche _____ %

b. Hurting Touch _____ %

c. Scary Touch _____ %

6. As a parent, the types of touch I give my child(ren) are:

a. Gentle_____

_____

b. Hurting _____

_____

c. Scary _____

_____

Touching Our Children

Children loved to be touched and held. It's a great way to increase parent-child bonding and positive emotional attachment that lasts a lifetime. Some children may experience discomfort while being touch or held, for example colicky children, or children with super high sensitivity to touch. Check with your medical doctor to learn more about the discomfort your child is experiencing. Find out ways that nurturing touch can still be a part of your relationship.

Touch is a basic need all people have. There are many ways parents and children can experience the pleasures of touch:

- Carry baby with you during your daily routines.

- Massage baby daily.

- Sit with baby on your lap.

- Lay with baby on the floor.

- Rub baby's body when changing diapers and clothes.

- Wash baby with warm water.

- Play with baby.

- Gently tickle baby.

- Touch baby's hands and feet.

- Dance and rock with your baby to music.

- Take turns dancing with your children.

- Exchange hugs with your children.

- Pat them on the back or rub their shoulders to encourage them.

- Greet and say good bye with a hug and kiss.

- If it's your custom to say grace at the table, hold hands.

- Give them a high five as a special recognition.

- Play games like riding a horse or airplane rides.

- Hold hands when sitting together.

- Play catch or tag where you get tickled when caught.

- Brush and arrange their hair.

- Invite them to lie on your lap for some cuddling.

- Play "patty cake" with your child.

- Blow raspberries on baby's belly, hands or feet.

Notes and Comments:

Family Home Practice Assignment

1. Practice giving gentle touch to your children each day. What ways did you give your children gentle touch this week?

   _____

   _____

   _____

   _____

   _____

2. Develop a routine for massaging your children every day. How did it go?

   _____

   _____

   _____

   _____

3. Praise your children at least two times each day.

   a. How did you praise your children for being? _____

   _____

   _____

   _____

   b. How did you praise your children for doing?_____

   _____

   _____

   _____

4. Do something to nurture yourself.

5. Spend a minimum of 30-45 nimutes each day playing, reading, and or massaging your child(ren).

Chapter 26

Time Out

Goal: *To increase parents' use of an effective alternative to spanking as aform of punishment.*

Time Out is a temporary isolation of a child from others when a child chooses to act inappropriately. It is a technique that lets children know that when they choose to behave inappropriately, they have to be by themselves for a while, sitting quietly.

Time Out is not solitary confinement in some dark room. It is not a threat of the loss of a parent's love or protection. Time Out is a temporary isolation of the child from others because they chose to act inappropriately.

115

When to Use Time Out

Use Time Out when the child seriously violates one or more of the family rules. Some examples may be:

- Deliberately breaking something.

- Throwing objects in the house in anger.

- Ignoring a repeated request to stop doing something.

- Abusive behaviors to others or to pets such as hitting, kicking, swearing, or pulling hair.

- Back talk; showing disrespect; acting offensive.

When Not to Use Time Out

Do not use Time Out for minor infractions of family rules, for behaviors you find partially annoying or unacceptable, or for normal accidents. Try ignoring the behavior or use another form of behavior modification instead of Time Out. The selected use of Time Out will increase its effectiveness as a management technique.

When to Begin Using Time Out

Time Out is an appropriate consequence to use when children are 2 ½ years and older. Infants and young toddlers should never be put in Time Out. They are simply too young to know right from wrong.

When Using Time Out, Never Do the Following...

- **Never** tell a child he has to sit in Time Out until he's ready to act like a human being.

He already is a human being and needs guidance, not sarcasm.

- **Never** tell a child you won't love him unless he cooperates and takes a Time Out. A parent's love is unconditional.

- **Never** tell a child to feel or think something you can't control. Statements like:

"You sit in Time Out until you feel sorry for what you did." Can you really monitor this feeling?

"I want you to think about what you did and what you'll do differently next time".

Fat chance that's going to happen. He's probably thinking at that moment he has the creepiest parents alive.

- **Never** threaten to use Time Out for everything inappropriate your child does.

- **Never** ask a child if he wants to take a Time Out. What normal child would answer yes?

When used sparingly and appropriately, Time Out is a very powerful technique in helping children learn to make good choices and practice appropriate behavior.

Before You Use Time Out …

1. **Have you tried other techniques to avoid a Time Out?** So many parents use Time Outs at the drop of a hat or threaten a Time Out for everything. This is just lazy parenting and will surely diminish the effectiveness of this technique. Have you tried re-direction, giving other choices, used humor? The less you use Time Out, the more effective it is.

2. **Make sure the child understands the concept of Time Out.** Before using Time Out as a form of punishment, make sure the child understands what Time Out is and what you expect once he is in Time Out.

3. **Establish Family Rules.** Family rules let all family members know what is acceptable and unacceptable behavior.

4. **Pick a Time Out place.** The area should be without interesting things to do or look at. Sending a child to their bedroom would not be an appropriate Time Out.

A child's bedroom has too many things to do (read, color, play) or look at (TV, magazines, pictures). Furthermore, a bedroom should be a child's sanctuary, a place to feel cozy and comfortable. If children's bedrooms are used as places for punishments, they may generalize their angry feelings to all the times they have to spend in their room. Since children already have a sufficient number of night fears, there is no sense in contributing any feelings of discomfort to a bedroom. A stairway (for children who can walk), hallway, or a chair near a wall, are all appropriate possibilities for a Time Out space. There's not much to do at these places except sit and wait. *NEVER lock a child in a room, or use a dark, scary room, or rooms without enough ventilation for Time Out.* Time Out is the removal of a child from a pleasant situation to a non-reinforcing situation. It is not a jail sentence.

5. **Establish how long the Time Out will be.** The precise amount of time depends on the age of the child and the seriousness of the offense. Less serious behaviors get one to two minutes of Time Out; more serious behaviors get three to seven minutes. Short duration Time Outs (one to seven minutes) are more effective than longer Time Outs (15-30 minutes).

How to Use Time Out

1. **Give the child one warning that the behavior is inappropriate, and if it continues, they will have to take a Time Out.** For example, you might say, "Tom, please stop acting silly at the dinner table and use proper table manners. If you continue to act silly, you will have to leave the dinner table and take a two-minute Time Out." Be supportive and factual - not threatening.

2. **If the inappropriate behavior continues, tell the child to go to the Time Out area.** If the child resists leaving, use minimum physical direction to ensure the departure to Time Out. Accomplish departure to Time Out by gently taking a child by their arm, or under both arms near the shoulder, and encouraging the child to take the Time Out. Never use abusive physical force to accomplish a Time Out. The consequence of the inappropriate behavior is lost in the abusive force and in the power struggle that will ensue.

3. **Ignore all comments, promises, or arguments by the child that she or he won't do the behavior anymore.** Any attention by the parent may reinforce the inappropriate behavior. Carry through the consequence to have the child take a Time Out.

4. **Tell the child how long the Time Out will last.** Be very specific. "Tom, you have a two-minute Time Out for acting silly at the dinner table after I gave you one warning. After two minutes of sitting quietly, you may return." It is not up to the child to determine when to return, or up to you to decide when you can stand the child again. Time Out is a formal consequence to a formal family rule. If you have a kitchen timer, it is a good way to be accurate and to meet the Time Out objective. Remember to ignore any inquiries about when Time Out is over.

5. **Remind the child that Time Out doesn't start until he or she is quiet.** If the child runs away from the Time Out place, take the child back to the Time Out place. Remind the child that the Time Out period begins when they are sitting quietly.

6. **After the Time Out is over, redirect the child to appropriate behaviors.** Praise the child for being quiet in Time Out. If you had to remove the child from the dinner table, allow the child to finish dinner. If the inappropriate behavior occurred during play time, spend a little time with the child modeling appropriate behavior for the play activity. If the inappropriate behavior occurs again, it is time to have a serious problem-solving discussion as to why the child is choosing to get into trouble.

Some Points to Consider

1. **Time Out works best with preschool and school-age children.** Time Out with teenagers is not a useful behavior modification technique. Other techniques such as choices and consequences, humor, and loss of privileges are more effective with adolescents.

2. **Time Out can be voluntary or involuntary.** A child can initiate a voluntary Time Out after an inappropriate behavior has taken place. An involuntary Time Out is when the parent requests that the child leave the area after some misdeed.

3. **Time Out is effective only when time in is quality time.** If the time spent together is not fun and pleasant for both the parent and child, Time Out will not be nearly as effective. Spend quality time with your children and Time Out won't need to be used that often.

4. **Time Out is a punishment for children - not for adults.** If family rules are established and a parent chooses to break one of the rules, taking a Time Out would not be an appropriate consequence. Time Out is a parenting strategy used by parents for children.

When adults violate family rules, other forms of punishment can be used such as fines, restitution, apologies, etc.

118

Family Home Practice Assignment

1. Discuss with your partner and/or others involved in the daily parenting of your children how and when Time Out will be used in your family.

2. Explain to your child(ren) the punishment of Time Out and how you will use it in the family.

3. If your child is 2 ½ years or older, and a serious misbehavior has occurred, practice using Time Out.

4. What was the outcome? _____

_____

_____

_____

_____

_____

_____

_____

_____

_____

_____

_____

5. Spend a minimum of 30-45 minutes each day playing, reading, and/or massaging your child(ren).

Chapter 27

Child Proofing Your House From Danger

Goal: *To increase parents' use of an effective alternative to spanking as a form of punishment.*

Child proofing is a term describing the actions parents take to make the living conditions of a house safe for a child.

Why Child Proof?

Children, especially young toddlers, love to explore. Touching, pulling, grabbing, and eating are just a few of the ways young children explore their environment. Since toddlers are generally too young to know what is safe to play with and what is potentially dangerous, parents child proof a house to protect children from becoming hurt, or in some instances, even killed. Child proofing prevents dangerous interactions.

120

Parents also child proof their house to enhance the positive interactions they have with their children. *A house where dangerous objects are out of reach is a house where parents aren't constantly saying "No"!*

Is Your House Child Proofed?

You probably wonder at times whether your house is safe enough for your toddler to play in without a high risk for injury. There are two things you can do to see if your house is safe for toddlers:

1. Get down on your hands and knees and view the world as a toddler. What you can pull, grab, bite, so can your child. Move tempting and dangerous objects out of reach.

2. Watch your child as he explores his environment. Walk with your child through the house and notice what he notices. Can he reach that shelf? Can he push that button? You'll soon find out by watching him. If he can reach objects he shouldn't, it's time to better child proof your house.

Once Child Proofed, Always Child Proofed?

Right? Wrong! Babies grow along with their ability to reach for objects, climb on furniture, open drawers, and walk up and down stairs. You will continually need to modify your house as your child continues to grow. The good news is that as your child grows older, he's also learning what is safe and what isn't.

Common Dangers

1. **Paint chips.** For young children, everything goes in their mouth. Many older homes have been painted with lead-based paint which can be toxic to young children.

2. **Cigarette butts.** Nicotine can kill a child if eaten.

3. **Plants.** Some plants can be poisonous.

4. **Open containers of alcohol, and beer cans.** Alcohol can cause permanent brain and liver damage to a young child.

5. **Cigarette lighters and matches.** Burns from cigarette lighters and matches are a common injury in preschoolers.

Family Home Practice Assignment

Use the Home Safety Checklists on the following pages to modify your home, making the house safe for your child to explore.

Notes and Comments:

121

Home Safety Checklist #1

The following checklist is designed to ensure your house is safe enough for your child to play in with only minimal risk of injury. Take some time now to go over this checklist, room by room, to make your house safe for your child. Make it a habit to recheck your house at least once a month.

Action Needed   **Check when completed**

ALL ROOMS

1. Put electric outlet covers on all unused outlets.   _____
2. Put a gate across all stairways, top and bottom, until child can handle stairs.   _____
3. Remove or pad sharp corners on furniture and appliances.   _____
4. Remove throw rugs on tiled floors.   _____
5. Use non-skid floor wax on wood, tile, or linoleum floors.   _____
6. Keep all plants out of baby's reach.   _____

KITCHEN

1. Put all cleaning supplies on a top shelf out of children's reach.   _____
2. Install safety locks on all kitchen cabinets below waist level. You may want to keep one cabinet with pots, pans, and unbreakable bowls unlocked for child's exploration.   _____
3. Turn pot handles toward back of stove when cooking. Use the back burners on stove for cooking.   _____
4. Take knobs off of gas range when not in use.   _____
5. Have a secure cover for the garbage can.   _____
6. Install safety locks on kitchen drawers with knives and other sharp utensils.   _____
7. Keep all breakable bowls out of the cabinets with the pots and pans.   _____
8. Remove throw rugs from kitchen floors.   _____

BASEMENT, GARAGE, ATTIC

1. Throw away all old paints you're not using. Store paint thinners, paint, stains, on a high shelf.   _____
2. Store all tools in a locked tool chest or shelved out of reach.   _____
3. Lock all doors securely.   _____
4. Keep garden tools, lawn mowers, snow blowers out of reach of young children.   _____
5. Keep keys to electric machines safely out of reach.   _____
6. Take doors off of old refrigerators and freezers.   _____
7. Store pesticides and fertilizers on high shelves out of reach of children.   _____

Home Safety Checklist #2

Action Needed   **Check when completed**

BATHROOM

1. Store all electrical appliances such as hair dryers, curling irons, etc. in the
    bathroom cabinet or closet.   _____
2. Put safety locks on all bathroom cabinets.   _____
3. Remove all electric appliances near water.   _____
4. Place a non-skid bath mat on the bottom of the tub.
5. Buy rubber safety covers for bathtub water faucets and spout to prevent accidental
    head injuries and scalding.   _____
6. Keep all medicine in a locked medicine cabinet.   _____
7. Always test the water before putting your child in the tub.   _____
8. Lower your water heater temperature to 110 degrees to prevent burning your child. _____

ROOM

1. Secure lamps and other freestanding objects.   _____
2. Fence off fireplaces, wood stoves, space heaters, radiators, and heating grates. _____
3. Remove all breakable knick-knacks and ashtrays.   _____
4. Keep guns out of the house. If guns are in the house, unload them, put them in a
    locked place and keep the keys out of your child's reach. Store the gun separate
    from the bullets.   _____
5. Attach electrical lamp cords and extension cords to tables or baseboards. _____
6. Remove coffee table and other sharp-edged furniture from child's access and
    play areas.   _____

BEDROOMS

1. Install a night light for nighttime trips to the bathroom.   _____
2. Move furniture and cribs away from windows. Corner posts of the crib should be
    level with the top of the rails.   _____
3. Place safety locks on all windows and screens.   _____
4. Make sure bars on cribs are no more than 2 3/8 inches apart.   _____
5. Make sure mattress fits bed frame snugly. No more than two fingers should
    fit in the space between the mattress and the sides of the crib. Place rolled
    towels between mattress and crib to fill space.   _____
6. Install bumper pads on inside of crib for young infants, the soft kind that bend.
    or fold when stood on.   _____
7. Remove bumpers, pillow and toys from crib if your baby can push up. _____
8. Remove mobiles over bed once child is capable of sitting or pulling to sit. _____

Driving With Your Children

Infant (birth to about 20-24 pounds): Infant or Convertible Safety Seat

- Always use rear-facing car seats or use an infant car bed. The safest place for the car seat is in the back seat of the vehicle.

- A rear-facing car seat cannot be used in the front seat with an air bag. A car bed, which lies flat, can be used with an air bag.

- If your baby is less than 6 pounds, talk to your health care provider about special positioning instructions or using a car bed.

- The harness should be threaded through the lower slots, just at or below the child's shoulders.

About 20-40 pounds: Forward-Facing Child Safety Seat

- The harness *must* be threaded through the top slots or the seat can break.

- The safest place for the car seat is in the back seat of the vehicle. If the child must ride in front with an air bag, adjust the vehicle seat as far back as possible.

30 - 60 pounds: Auto Booster Seat

- A belt-positioning auto booster seat offers better upper body restraint for your child.

- A belt-positioning booster *must* be used with a lap and shoulder belt.

- You must use a shield booster if you have only a lap belt.

- The safest place for the booster seat is in the back seat of the vehicle.

General Safety Rules

1. Never leave a young child unattended in the bathroom.
2. Install smoke alarms and fire extinguishers.
3. Keep all matches and candles out of reach.
4. Post emergency numbers beside the telephone.
5. Never refer to medication as candy.
6. Avoid letting children play with small objects they can swallow.
7. Never leave a young child unattended in the basement, garage, or attic.
8. Keep ashtrays and cigarette butts out of children's reach. Nicotine is a deadly poison when eaten.
9. Keep plastic bags and deflated or burst balloons away from young children.
10. Keep alcohol and cigarettes away from young children.
11. Use toddler gates at the top and bottom of stairs.
12. Lock matches and lighters in a cabinet that is higher than your shoulders.

Safety Reminders by Age

1 month: Crib Check. Make sure there is no space between mattress and crib side for baby to get caught. Use bumper pads.

2 months: Guard Against Falls. Babies can roll over already. Never leave a child unattended on a dressing table or other high place. Always use a properly installed car seat. If you also use the seat outside of the car, prevent falls by never putting it above floor level.

4 months: Guard Against Choking. Do not give young children small objects or pieces of hard food such as peanuts, popcorn, or hard candy. Learn the approved anti-choking maneuver for children from your pediatrician.

5 months: Guard Against Scalds. Babies like to grab and hit at things in your hands. Do not drink or carry hot liquids when near or holding a baby.

6 months: Sitting Alone. Baby may sit alone - but not in the bathtub. Never leave a child unattended in or near water.

7 months: Safe Exploring. Keep dangerous or breakable objects up and out of young crawler's exploring reach.

8 months: Pulling Up. Watch for falls. Check crib for areas where baby may catch his head or neck.

9 months: Avoid Shocks. Block electrical plugs with approved safety devices.

10 months: Bigger Car Seat. Switch to a toddler car seat and use it every time the child is in the car.

11 months: Burns. In the kitchen, hot liquids, grease, and hot foods are a danger. So are irons, hot stoves, radiators, heating registers, and fireplaces.

12 months: Stairway Safety. Watch for open doors and stairs. Use gates at the top and bottom of steps.

13 months: Walking and Exploring. Beware of poisoning danger from houseplants, household chemicals, and medicines. Keep poison control phone number, and first aid chart and supplies handy.

14 months: Climbing. Children can now climb on chairs and tables - and find more danger. Keep medications and cleaning fluids out of reach. Use safety tops on all bottles and jars. Put locks on cabinets and drawers.

16 months: Exploring Outdoors. Define play areas and make them safe and interesting. Guard against scratches and bites from stray cats and dogs.

18 months: Water Play. Never leave a child alone in a tub or near any quantity of water - even a pail or a puddle - even if the child has had "swimming" lessons.

2 years Expanding Limits: Start teaching good pedestrian habits and the limits of the child's "territory."

3 years: Riding a Tricycle. Driveways and streets are dangerous. Allow riding only in fenced yards or playgrounds.

4 years: Venturing Further. Teach good pedestrian habits - look both ways, stay out from between parked cars.

5 years: Bigger and Bigger. You can now switch to seat belts for your child. Don't forget to "buckle up" yourself every time, too.

6 years: Riding a Bicycle. Watch for falls. Teach good bicycle and street safety. Don't forget the bike helmet.

Notes and Comments:

Chapter 28

Verbal and Physical Redirection

Redirection is a parenting technique to help children learn appropriate behavior.

- Redirection is used by parents to:

- Prevent personal injury.

- Promote desirable behavior.

- Reducing punishing interactions.

- Promote learning and exploration.

Goal: ***To increase parents' use of verbal and physical redirection as a behavior management technique***

Verbal Redirection

Verbal redirection is a way of managing your child's behavior by verbally expressing a command or request. It is a way of redirecting the behavior of your child by talking to him. A parent tells a child that the behavior that is occurring, or is about to occur, is not acceptable. A statement telling the child what is acceptable follows.

Appropriate Examples:

- "Chairs are for sitting. No standing, please."

- "No standing in the tubby. Sit, please."

- "Oh what a nice toy. Put it back on the shelf, please."

Inappropriate Examples:

- "No standing on the chair. You'll fall and break your neck."

- "Quit standing in the tub. What do you want, an accident?"

- "Yes, I see your toy. Now just don't leave it on the floor."

From these examples, you can see that the appropriate use of verbal redirection helps the child know what the parent expects and doesn't expect. The inappropriate use of verbal redirection actually doesn't redirect a child's behavior at all. Threats, statements of doom, and telling a child what not to do are not the correct ways to use verbal redirection
Verbal redirection also includes directing the child's attention and behavior to other more appropriate activities and avoiding unnecessary confrontations.

Example: Adam is about to run out of the bedroom when mom is trying to finish dressing him. She calls out, "Adam, close the door for mom, please." Adam's attention is redirected from running away and he ends up complying and feeling like a helper.
This type of redirection works well with toddlers who haven't yet figured out that they are being redirected. It is not as effective after the age of three years.

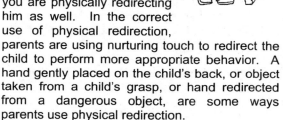

Physical Redirection

Physical redirection is similar to verbal redirection with one added feature. As you are verbally redirecting a child, you are physically redirecting him as well. In the correct use of physical redirection, parents are using nurturing touch to redirect the child to perform more appropriate behavior. A hand gently placed on the child's back, or object taken from a child's grasp, or hand redirected from a dangerous object, are some ways parents use physical redirection.

Appropriate Examples:

- Physical redirecting a child away from an electric socket to a safe toy to play with.

- Escorting a child from the bathroom to the living room and engaging the child in play.

- Taking a dangerous object away from a child and substituting it with a safer one.

127

Inappropriate Examples:

- Physically jerking a child away from the electric socket.

- Spanking a child for entering the bathroom unassisted.

- Slapping a child's hand for touching a dangerous object.

In the appropriate use of physical redirection, a parent is using nurturing touch. In the inappropriate use of physical redirection, harsh and abusive touch is being used. The young preschool child is unable to make the connection between the harsh physical touch administered by the parent, and the danger to the object being touched. In the Nurturing Program, we believe the use of hitting, slapping, spanking, and other forms or harsh touch are abusive and have no positive value in helping a child learn appropriate behaviors.

Verbal and Physical Redirection Used Together

The ideal way to redirect a child's behavior is through the combined use of verbal and physical redirection. Used together, the child quickly learns that a particular behavior is unacceptable to his parents.

How to Use Verbal and Physical Redirection

1. In a firm voice, let the child know he is performing or about to perform an unacceptable behavior. The firm voice indicates this is not a game; the "No" indicates he is to stop the behavior immediately.

2. Approach the child, stoop down, make eye contact, and hold his hands.

3. Tell the child his behavior is unacceptable. Use words like, "icky," or "ouch," or "hot" if he is near something that could injure him like an electric socket, or hot oven. Use other words if the child has something in his hand, or is touching something you prefer him not touching. Words like, "No," or "This is Mommy's; not for Billy," or "Sorry, this is not for little boys," convey the message. Used consistently, a child will begin to associate these words with certain behaviors.

4. Attempt to let the child re-establish the original setting. That is, if he has taken something, physically and verbally redirect him to return the object to where it belongs. If he has turned on an appliance, have him turn the appliance off. In this instance, you are encouraging the child to perform behaviors that are pleasing to you. Children like to please their parents.

5. The next step is the use of physical and verbal redirection. The goal is not to inhibit a child's natural curiosity, but to foster it through more appropriate activity. Engage the child in play. Some things children like are:

   - Keys and locks

   - Putting anything smaller into something bigger

   - Puzzles

   - Coloring/scribbling on paper.

Make the activity you want the child to engage in so exciting that the child can't help but join you.

6. Praise the child for cooperating. Tell him he is a good listener. Praise for doing will reinforce future encounters. After all, you want your child to listen and cooperate.

7. If the child chooses to perform the inappropriate behavior again, repeat steps 1 through 6. A child is likely to repeat the behavior for two reasons: young children are too young to remember what was bad or good; and, some preschool children are likely to test you and the rule for consistency.

128

8. Physical redirection is usually necessary and is more effective with younger children when their language is not as well developed. Physical redirection should always be used with some form of verbal redirection. Also, physical redirection is used less as children get older, understand language better, and want to be independent.

Some added advice:

1. Never hit or spank a child as a means of physical redirection. Hitting is an abusive practice that sends a double message: "I'm concerned about your safety, but I hit you and cause you pain and fear."

2. We caution parents in the use of the word, "NO." Because toddlers like to explore, their whole world can become one big "No-No" if you let it. Save "No" for the big things. Also, when you use the word "No," show an expression of disapproval. Slowly turning the head from side to side (physical indicator of No) and a cold, non-smiling face tells the child you are displeased. After a while, just shaking your head "no" gets the message across.

3. Child proof your house. Get all the valued objects, CD players, statues, etc. above your child's grasp level. Life will be easier for you and your child.

4. If your child continues to want to perform the unacceptable behavior despite your efforts, it may be necessary to take the child to another room, or to spend more time with the child to "take his mind off whatever he wanted to touch."

5. Finally, be consistent. A "No" is a "No" every time the unacceptable behavior appears. If you're inconsistent in the application of your redirection, expect your child to be the same. Spend the time and energy now in being consistent. You and your child will find living together an enjoyable experience.

Family Home Practice Assignment

1. Practice using verbal and physical redirection during the week.

2. Describe a situation: _____

   _____

   _____

   _____

   _____

   _____

   _____

   _____

3. Have you completed the Home Safety Checklists?

4. Praise your child at least two times each day: once for Being and once for Doing.

5. Spend a minimum of 30-45 minutes each day playing, reading, and/or massaging your child(ren).

Notes and Comments:

Chapter 29

Establishing Nurturing Parenting Routines

Nurturing parenting routines are very important in creating a warm and caring home. A routine is a certain way of doing something. Everyone incorporates routines into their daily lives from getting dressed to going to bed. Routines put order into our lives and, in turn, make our lives easier and more predictable. Nurturing parenting routines help children by providing them with a consistent, predictable and caring way of life.

Our goal as parents of young children is to establish nurturing parenting routines to make our job as a parent a little easier, and to make their job of being a child more fun and reassuring.

Goal: *To increase parents' awareness of the importance of establishing nurturing parenting routines.*

130

In all the research conducted over the years on child development, four important factors stand out related to the health of young children:

1. Feelings of trust and security;

2. Demonstrating caring for oneself and for others;

3. A strong sense of personal power; and

4. Feelings of positive self worth.

Feelings of Trust and Security

Nurturing parenting routines help establish feelings of security and trust in children. Children love to know what is going to happen to them. Questions like, "Are we almost there yet?" and "How much longer?" and "Is it going to hurt?" and the ever present "Why?" are all requests for information to help children organize their world. Adults like to know what's going on - why shouldn't children?

Children feel secure when they know what to expect and are treated in a respectful manner. Feelings of security help children learn to trust their parents and other caring family members. When children learn to trust others, they learn to trust themselves. As they continue to mature into adolescents and adults, they become secure and trustworthy people in their own right, then pass these traits on to their children. The circle is now complete and the world becomes a little more caring and secure place to live.

Empathy - The Ability to Care

Empathy is the ability to be aware of the needs and feelings of another person and respond in a caring, respectful manner. Empathy is truly one of the greatest gifts a parent can give their children. To demonstrate empathy is to demonstrate caring. Research clearly shows that empathic children are more popular in school, are more outgoing, more sensitive and better adjusted emotionally than children with low levels of empathy. Nurturing parenting routines used in a consistent manner will clearly help children experience and value the qualities of empathy.

Personal Power

Nurturing parenting routines encourage children to be active participants in their daily care. Giving children choices, honoring their opinions and feelings, and encouraging their growth and independence all contribute to the ongoing development of a child who feels respected and empowered.

While many parents shudder at the thought of fostering a sense of personal power in young children, it's a well accepted conclusion that children who feel they have a sense of personal power don't engage in ongoing power struggles and tend to be more cooperative, contributing members of their family.

Children with a strong, positive sense of personal power are also less likely to engage in unhealthy and destructive behaviors such as violence towards self and others, drugs and alcohol.

131

In a child's world of repeated pressures by their peer group, having personal power is the best protection a child can have.

Feelings of Positive Self Worth

Children who have a positive self worth generally display a positive, healthy outlook on life, treat themselves and others with respect and make good choices.

Feelings of Positive Self Worth

Children who have a positive self worth generally display a positive, healthy outlook on life, treat themselves and others with respect and make good choices.

When any element of life has worth, it has value. When some thing has value, it is treasured.

A positive self-worth is an emotional insurance program for children which acts as a safety net for the rough times that life has to offer. Positive self-worth promotes a healthy quality of life.

Establishing Nurturing Parenting Routines

There are several important ingredients that go into establishing nurturing parenting routines.

- **Gentle Touch.** Gentle positive touch such as hugs of comfort and hugs of joy, kisses, tickles and massages communicate love and caring to your child. Gentle touch is such an important part of parenting. Did you know that if a baby is not touched in a positive consistent way their body and brain will stop growing?

  After years of studying how babies grow, we now know that physically stroking a baby will

help them digest their food better and will also help the premature child gain weight more quickly. Regularly massaging your baby also significantly lowers their stress hormones, not to mention the feelings of closeness both parent and child experience.

It's easy to see why touch is an important ingredient in all your nurturing parenting routines.

- **Praising your Child.** As you are learning in the Nurturing Program, praising your children and the good things they do build their sense of power, their self-worth, and the desire to cooperate. Statements like, "What a sweet boy you are!" tells your son his very being is appreciated by you and "Good job eating your food!" tells him you're pleased with his efforts.

- **Happy Pleasant Facial Expressions.** Young children love to look at a happy, playful face. Actually, given the option, most adults would rather look at a happy, playful face than a grumpy, mean-looking face. Mean faces scare kids and hardly make the experience a "Kodak moment."

- **Having a Sense of Caring.** Caring is the cornerstone to nurturing parenting routines. From extensive studies, we know an infant's brain is a work in progress. Just like talking to and reading to a child helps develop the part of the brain responsible for language and thinking, caring helps develop the part of the child's brain that is responsible for the emotions children express.

- A nurturing, caring environment can strengthen a young child's emotional stability and have a long-lasting effect on them for the rest of their lives.

- **Having Fun and a Sense of Humor**. There is nothing like a sense of humor to help a parent and a child through a day. Humor doesn't mean poking fun at children or saying something embarrassing. A sense of humor is a feeling that happiness and playfulness are important aspects of life.

Parents who are under a lot of stress and who have neglected their own needs will find very little to be happy about. Make a commitment to bring laughter and fun into your relationship with your children.

Nurturing routines can be established for many of the daily tasks you and your young child experience such as:

- Diapering and Dressing Times;
- Feeding times;
- Bath Times; and
- Bedtime

Parents should begin to establish nurturing routines the moment they bring their baby home. Starting early is the best way to establish consistent, caring and loving parent-child

interactions. The Nurturing Program helps parents learn to establish nurturing routines with their children, ages birth to five years. The next four chapters provide information on how to establish nurturing parenting routines.

Family Home Practice Assignment

1. Meet with your partner and others who are a critical part of raising your child to review the practice of nurturing routines.

2. Praise yourself once a day.

3. Spend a minimum of 30-45 minutes each day playing, reading, and/or massaging your child(ren).

Notes and Comments:

Chapter 30

Establishing a Nurturing Diapering and Dressing Routine

Goal: ***To increase parents' ability to implement a nurturing parenting diapering and dressing routine***

Diapering and dressing children are excellent times to use nurturing routines. During these times, parents can be encouraging enormous growth in the child's sense of independence and cooperation, as well as in positive nurturing touch. Let's take a closer look at how parents can establish nurturing diapering and dressing routines.

134

Autonomy and Cooperation

Children like to do things for themselves as quickly as they can. You can see it very early when infants repeatedly try to stand and walk only to fall flat on their bottoms. You can also see it when they attempt to feed themselves by smearing food all over their faces with the hope that some if it will get in their mouths.

Little successes in these and other tasks result in great joy because children are finally learning to do things for themselves. These accomplishments have great value in that they help foster in children their feelings of personal power and positive self worth. These accomplishments also foster feelings of autonomy and cooperation. After all, in order to smear the food all over your face, someone has to bring it to you.

Cooperation is established very early in the parent-child relationship. Just as in eating, dressing and diapering children is a partnership between the parent and the child. As a partnership, you and your children work together as a team in getting clothes on and off your child. The following steps are offered to foster this partnership.

1. **Let your children have input into what they will wear for the day.** You might do this by selecting two tops and two bottoms and having your child make a choice of which top and bottom to wear. In this way, your child is taking an active role in getting dressed. Also, in a partnership your child needs to take an active role in getting dressed and undressed rather than the passive role most children experience. Too many parents dress and undress their child without the child's active assistance. The active partnership role builds autonomy and cooperation.

2. **Allow your children to do the things they can do by themselves without any help from you.** If they can put their socks on, fine, let them do it by themselves. If it's pulling up their pants, good, don't do it for them. Let them pull their own pants up. Allow them extra time to complete the task.

3. **Assist your children in getting dressed but when necessary, allow them to still have the lead.** In this step, you're only assisting your children in doing things they can't quite do alone yet. Infants need a lot of assistance; toddlers need some; preschoolers hardly need any help.

4. **Take the lead in assisting your children in getting dressed by doing the things they are incapable of doing.** In the last step, you do the things your children are incapable of doing. It might be putting on and tying shoes, zipping zippers, buttoning buttons, etc. In step four, the child has yet to develop the skills to finish getting dressed that one day he will have. As your child develops more skills, the need for step four is less and less.

To assist you in knowing what steps to use and when to use them, here are some suggestions.

- Observe your child and make it a point to know what your child is capable of doing independently. The younger the child, the more quickly these skills will change on a daily and weekly basis.

135

- When you are pretty sure of the tasks your child can do by himself, break the tasks he can't do into smaller steps. The smaller steps will allow him to continue to gain further feelings of confidence. Let's take the activity of putting on a pair of pants. First, have him sit in a chair without you placing him there if he can do it by himself. Second, gather the pant legs and make doughnuts and lay them on the floor just in front of his feet. Third, tell him to step into the holes and ease the pants around his ankles. Fourth, have him take hold of one or both sides and "pull up." If he is very young, he probably doesn't have strength to pull the pants up all the way so you will have to help. Fifth, you do the snapping of the pants if it's something he can't do by himself.

Babies participate in the partnership method of getting dressed and many parents aren't even aware of it. When babies are getting their diapers changed, many children participate in the partnership method by lying still while mom or dad is putting a clean diaper on the child. Although this level of partnership may seem slight for the developmental level of the child, it is indeed very active.

Young children also are active participants in getting themselves dressed by holding their arms and legs up, and by putting their arms through the sleeve openings. If you keep a sharp eye open, you'll notice all the things your young infant can do with a little assistance.

There you have it, the partnership method of helping your child get dressed. It takes a lot more time than getting your child dressed while they stand passively waiting for you to finish. However, the time you spend in establishing a nurturing dressing routine when your child is young will pay off later when your child is more capable, cooperative, and independent.

Family Home Practice Assignment

1. Practice implementing the nurturing diapering and dressing routine with your children each day.

2. Spend a minimum of 30-45 minutes each day playing, reading, and/or massaging your child(ren).

Notes and Comments:

Chapter 31

Establishing a Nurturing Feeding Time Routine

Goal: *To increase parents' ability to implement a nurturing parenting feeding time routine*

Eating is one of the most pleasurable times during infancy and childhood. Babies love to eat. In fact, most babies double their birth weigh in the first three to five months of life. That's a lot of eating! If they could talk, babies would probably tell us that nothing in this world is as good as sucking on a nipple and getting milk or juice. Watch them when they are eating: they relax, begin to coo, close their eyes and fall asleep. Just like adults, only we have recliners. Parents are pleased when babies eat because the child quiets down and is more pleasant to be with later when they wake up.

As children begin to grow older, something happens that changes all this pure pleasure into frustration, dissatisfaction, and stress for both the children and the parents.

Children refuse to eat certain foods, snack between meals and begin to hate the very foods the parents feel are the best for them.

The Importance of Feeding Times

To begin to understand how feeding and eating begin to go sour, let's first discuss some common facts about children's eating habits.

- Despite some popular beliefs, babies know how many calories they need and what their stomachs can handle. If babies are not getting enough, they'll want more. If they get too much, they will stop sucking and eating. A child who turns his head away is telling his parents "I'm full!"

- Feeding is one of the earliest experiences babies have. As such, they begin to learn a lot about themselves and the world they live in. Good experiences in feeding lead to good feelings of themselves and their world. Bad experiences lead to bad feelings about themselves and their world.

- Babies will normally lose weight immediately after birth, but gradually begin to gain back lost weight in two or three days. Such losses in weight are to be expected.

- Somewhere around a year old, babies begin to change their feelings about food. They become choosier and less hungry. What might look good to eat today won't look good tomorrow. Their choice of certain foods is the beginning of exerting autonomy and control of their lives.

- Teething often takes away children's appetites, especially when the first molars are beginning to come in.

- As children become more mobile (around one year), they may lose interest in eating because they often feel too busy exploring the environment and practicing new motor skills to sit still and eat.

Establishing a Nurturing Feeding Time Routine

The following steps are offered to make feeding your child a more pleasant experience.

1. **Provide your child with a comfortable eating environment.** Putting young babies in infant seats and older children in high chairs securely stationed on a table or the floor, helps provide the child with feelings of security. Padded cushions and straps to keep your child snug in the seat are essential.

2. **Allow your child the opportunity to reject food.** When you honor their actions, you are reinforcing feelings of personal power. Remember, children know when they are not hungry, or when they don't like something just like you and I do. When you force your child to take "one more bite" of food he doesn't want, you're actually setting up a conflict situation in which the child will end up the loser.

3. **Reinforce personal choice in eating.** Get in the habit of giving small portions. If the child wants more, he'll let you know. Making children sit at the table until they clean their plates does not build healthy attitudes toward eating.

4. **Try to get children to think of food as something they want, not something they**

need to reject. One way to encourage positive attitudes toward food is to allow your child to eat larger than usual amounts of one wholesome food than others. Remember, the older the child gets, the more his attitudes and tastes are changing. Continue to offer servings of your child's less preferred foods but don't expect your child to enjoy these foods as his favorites.

5. **Encourage your child to begin to feed himself around nine to ten months.** Practice with finger foods, bread crusts, and other foods. Children will want to pick up the food with their fingers. Let them. Expect a lot of accidental messes. If you're worried about the rug, put some plastic under the highchair.

6. **Encourage your child to use a spoon.** Give him reason to use it. At the beginning of the meal when he's the hungriest, let him try to get food on the spoon and into his mouth.

7. **Don't worry about table manners.** Touching, smashing, squeezing, and smearing food is an early form of child's play. Don't punish your child or take his food away. Remember, building positive attitudes toward food and eating is nearly as important as the actual eating of the food.

8. **Praise your child.** There are many behaviors you can praise: feeding himself, eating a wholesome meal, sitting patiently waiting for food, using a fork or spoon, wiping his face, etc. Remember, praise the behavior you want.

Take some time to remember the eating experiences you had as a child. There is a tendency for parents to repeat these practices whether we liked them or not. Developing a nurturing parenting routine around feeding will make the experience of eating a positive one for you and your child.

Family Home Practice Assignment

1. Practice implementing the nurturing feeding routine with each of your children.

2. Continue implementing the nurturing routine for diapering and dressing.

3. Spend a minimum of 30-45 minutes each day playing, reading, and/or massaging your child(ren).

Notes and Comments:

Copyright 2009   Family Development Resources, Inc.   www.nurturingparenting.com   1-800-688-5822

Chapter 32

Feeding Your Young Children Nutritious Foods

Goal: *Increase parents awareness regarding nutritious foods for their children.*

Yuck! I am not eating that!

When meal time comes around, our children can have very different kinds of reactions. What most discourages us as parents though is when it seems like they make a face at everything. The following are some ideas and lists of suggestions for snacks and meals for your little ones. Please, be creative in your kitchen and feel free to add your own flavor to the ideas presented, be it Caribbean, Central, South American or another.

Typical foods such as soups, broths, meat and rice dishes as well as salads etc., can offer nourishing and balanced nutrition for our children, as long as we avoid too much fat, fried foods, and excessive sugar and salt. Now, before you get all somber and say, "Aw, but that's what makes our food so delicious," remember that if we are searching for good nutrition, thereby establishing in our children habits for life, as parents we have to be the ones to model these habits. We can help expose and educate our children's palettes, but we have start early!

With regards to vegetables, these tend to be the most rejected, and a good strategy is camouflage, including them in soups, purees, shakes or smoothies. Anything cut small (so little hands can manipulate them) and/or decorated with a fun appearance is more likely to tempt even the pickiest eater. You can also use cookie cutters to cut sandwich bread slices or fruit into geometric shapes (little triangles, circles, etc) *Have Fun!*

Nutritious Foods for Children – Quick and Easy!

Vegetable and Fruit Group

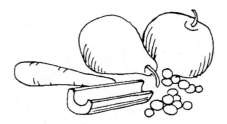

- Apples, peaches, pears, grapes, etc.

- Raw vegetable sticks or pieces (radishes, celery, cauliflower, green onions, zucchini, green peppers, carrots, cucumbers - even parsnips!).

- Dried apricots, raisins, prunes.

- Canned fruits or fruit juices kept chilled in the refrigerator.

- Mini-kabobs of bite-sized fruit chunks, strung on pretzel sticks.

- Banana chunks dipped in orange juice. Shake in a bag with chopped peanuts. Spear on pretzel sticks.

- Celery stuffed with cottage cheese, cheese spread or peanut butter.

- Juice cubes you make by freezing fruit juices in an ice cube tray.

- Tomato half, sprinkled with breadcrumbs, Parmesan or grated cheddar cheese and broiled.

- Creative salads of lettuce, raw spinach and other fresh vegetables, fruits, meats, eggs, or seafood.

Bread and Cereal Group

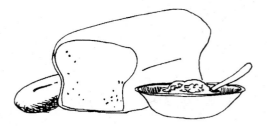

- Raisin bread toasted and spread with peanut butter.

- Sandwiches using a variety of breads - raisin, cracked wheat, pumpernickel, rye, black.

- Date-nut roll or brown bread spread with cream cheese.

- English muffins, served open-faced sandwiches such as hot roast beef or turkey, chicken salad, sloppy joes.

- Individual pizzas. Top English muffin halves with cheese slices, tomato sauce and oregano, and broil.

- Waffles topped with whipped topping and strawberries.

- Wheat or rye crackers topped with herb-seasoned cottage cheese, cheese or meat spread, or peanut butter.

- Graham crackers and milk.

- Ready-to-eat cereals right out of the box – provide cereals low in sugar.

- Ice cream or pudding, sprinkled with crisp cereals or wheat germ.

Meat, Poultry, Fish and Beans Group

- Nuts, sesame seeds, or toasted sunflower seeds.

- Sandwich spread of peanut butter combined with raisins or chopped dates.

- Peanut butter and honey spread on an English muffin, sprinkled with chopped walnuts, and heated under the broiler.

- Grilled open-faced peanut butter and mashed banana sandwich.

- Tomatoes stuffed with egg salad.

- Melon wedges topped with thinly sliced ham.

- Sandwich of cheese, meat, tomato, onion, and lettuce.

- Antipasto of tuna, shrimp, anchovies, hard cooked eggs and assorted vegetables.

- Leftover poultry or meat - as is, or chopped into a sandwich spread.

- Bite-sized cubes of broiled beef.

Milk and Cheese Group

- Milk shakes with mashed fresh berries or bananas.

- Parfait of cottage cheese, yogurt, or ice milk combined with fruit, sprinkled with chopped nuts, wheat germ, or crisp cereal.

- Dips for vegetable sticks. For fewer calories, substitute cottage cheese or plain yogurt for sour cream and mayonnaise in preparing dips.

- Fruit-flavored yogurt.

- Cheese cubes, or cheese cubes speared with pretzel sticks, or alternated with mandarin orange sections on a toothpick.

- Custard or pudding.

- Ice milk sundae, topped with fresh, canned, or frozen fruits.

Tips for Cooking With Children

You are the model; don't let your likes and dislikes influence the selection of food experiences.

1. Encourage the consumption of a variety of wholesome foods through positive experiences with foods.

2. Stress food in its natural state. Allow children to see, smell, feel, and taste the food at different stages of preparation. Compare colors and textures, shapes and sizes.

3. Choose simple cooking experiences first. As children master basic manipulative skills, gradually add more learning steps.

4. Develop "picture recipes," including utensils and illustrated measurement of ingredients.

5. Review the recipe and all directions before beginning a food activity.

6. Have all utensils ready ahead of time.

7. Sanitation: Does everyone have clean hands? Wash hands and work surface before starting. Explain what to do if child has to sneeze or cough.

8. Safety: Teach awareness of sharp objects and hot surfaces. Children use knives and graters only under close supervision.

9. Supervision: Recommendation of one adult to every five to six children.

10. Planning: Coordinate cooking with the class day. Build a food experience into multi-learning experiences - math, art, science, language, social science, safety, courtesy, and nutrition.

Family Home Practice Assignment

1. Do one thing to make family dinner time nicer.

2. Serve nutritious Snacks.

3. Spend a minimum of 30-45 minutes each day playing, reading, and/or massaging your child(ren).

Notes and Comments:

Source: Nutrition Education and Training Program,
Food and Nutrition Services Section,
Wisconsin Department of Public Instruction.

Chapter 33

Nurturing Bath Time Routine

Goal: *To increase parents' ability to implement a nurturing bath time routine.*

For many young children, getting into a bathtub of warm water is not one of their favorite things to do. But, almost all children love to walk in puddles, splash water on others, and run through open sprinklers. So why is bath time a time of frustration, tears, and stress for the children and their parents? Let's examine why.

There are several reasons why your son or daughter may experience bath time as a bad time.

- **Most bath times come at the end of the day.** Not only may young children be overtired, but parents may be feeling the stress of their day and communicate this stress by being a bit more demanding that their children cooperate. Children easily pick up on the parent's stress and become stressed themselves.

- **Because taking a bath comes at the end of the day, bath time is usually followed by bed time.** Children soon learn that taking a bath means soon they will have to go to bed. If a child wishes to stay up longer, the obvious is to resist taking a bath.

- **Many parents treat bath time as a chore rather than a time for fun, relaxation, and enjoyment.** An attitude of "having to take a bath" is established rather than an attitude of "wanting to take a bath."

- **The experience of taking a bath may be a very unpleasant and frightening one for many children.** Soap in eyes, hot water burns, accidental falls, pouring water on a child's head to rinse hair shampoo, etc. are all things that can make bath time a bad time.

- **Bath time for children in some families is often an "on again-off again" occurrence.** Sometimes children have to take baths, sometimes they don't. Although parents may have good rationale for excluding bath time, children, especially young children, don't understand why on some days they have to take a bath and on other days they don't. What they experience is inconsistency. This leads to feelings of anxiety, which is then exhibited as resistance.

Toddlers and Preschoolers

For children to want to take a bath more often than not, bath time has to be a fun time. The following suggestions are offered for developing a positive, nurturing routine for children's bath times.

1. **Make bath time sound like a fun time.** Young children like to pretend; give the bathtub a name or refer to it as "tubby time" with a sound of happiness. Pretend the tubby can talk and call the child's name, "Julia, I'm waiting for you" and answer back, "We're coming tubby." It's quite a bit better than saying, "Julia, I want you to take your bath now!"

2. **With parental supervision, let your child turn the water on and fill the tub.** Giving the child more responsibility in keeping himself clean is the ultimate goal. Start early by allowing him to put the bubble bath in, set the water temperature, and fill the tub

145

to the desired depth. Once again, parental supervision is required to ensure the temperature of the water is appropriate.

3. **Encourage your child to play in the tub.** Bring in "tubby toys" for the child to play with; they don't have to be anything fancy. Use plastic cups, bowls, empty plastic dish detergent containers, or plastic syrup containers with the plastic pour spouts, etc. Anything that floats, squirts water, holds, or pours water will work. Do not let your child have anything that can injure him if it is dropped or if it breaks. Heavy objects or sharp objects are clearly no-no's for children to play with. So is any glass product. If it's not made of foam or soft plastic - it's not an appropriate tubby toy.

4. **Encourage your child to get to know his/her body.** Tubby time is a great time for body exploration and recognition of body parts. Give your child's body parts names and use the names when washing your child: "Look I see Adam's hands. Oh, Boy! Adam's hands need a washing."

5. **Take a bath with your child(ren).** Children think it's great fun taking a bath with their mom or dad. Singing, playing with toys, and washing all help the child feel more comfortable when mom or dad are also in the tub.

6. **Make the experience of tubby time enjoyable.** Several things you can do to help make the experience of taking a bath more enjoyable:

- Use mild soaps and shampoos to avoid eye sting.

- Place a mat on the bottom of the tub to prevent accidental slipping.

- Protect against accidents by placing foam rubber guards over the water spout.

- Get each of your children their own towel to dry themselves and their own robe to wear after taking a bath.

7. **Make tubby time a routine of the day.** Depending on the age and activity, children may have to take a tubby everyday. Proper hygiene is an important value for children to learn. Washing does reduce the chance of germs being transmitted and infections spreading.

8. **Help children step out of the tub onto a dry towel or rug.** Floors with water on them can be as slippery as ice. The risk of falling on a slippery floor is much too high to chance. Have a dry towel or rug for your child to step on.

9. **Help your child dry off and use the time to have fun.** Be creative.

10. **Finish the bath time by rubbing lotion on your child.** Or, use the time to offer your child a massage. It's a special time between parent and child that only lasts a few years. Before you know it, your child places a high value on privacy and modesty and these fun tubby times are a memory.

Words of Caution

- Never, ever, leave a very young child alone in the bathtub. Accidental drowning and other injuries can occur in a matter of minutes and seconds. Infants and toddlers should never, ever be left alone.

- Keep all electrical appliances unplugged and away from the grasp of children. Water and electricity are deadly together. For the sake of your family's welfare, keep all electrical appliances safely stored in a locked cabinet or closet.

- Standing in a tub is an accident waiting to happen. Make it a family rule: No standing in the tub during tubby time. Sitting or kneeling is okay.

- Check the temperature of the hot water heater to ensure a safe level of heat to prevent burning.

Family Home Practice Assignment

1. Practice implementing the nurturing bath time routine with each of your children.

2. Continue to practice other nurturing routines for feeding, diapering and dressing.

3. Spend a minimum of 30-45 minutes each day playing, reading, and/or massaging your child(ren).

Notes and Comments:

Chapter 34

STDs, AIDS, and HIV

Sexually Transmitted Diseases (STDs)

- STDs are sexually transmitted diseases.

- One out of every 47 teens who are sexually active will get a STD.

- HIV or Human Immunodeficiency virus is an STD which is the base infection for AIDS.

- There may be as many as 20-30 STDs affecting sexually active people.

- On the average, two young people get HIV every hour in the United States.

- Some of the most common STDs today are: Chlamydia, Gonorrhea, Syphilis, Genital Herpes, Genital Warts, Trichomoniasis, AIDS.

- You cannot tell if someone has HIV or another STD just by their looks. Many STDs have no signs.

- Genital herpes is a common STD. It is an infection caused by the herpes simplex virus. Many people mistake it for a simple skin irritation. Genital herpes is a common infection nationwide with nearly 45 million people ages 12 and older infected.

- Many people, some males but mostly females, have no symptoms of a STD and may transmit the infection to a partner without knowing they are infected.

Goal: **To increase awareness of STDs, AIDS, and HIV prevention.**

148

- STDs can be passed from woman to a child during her pregnancy or during birth.

- Individuals who are sexually active should be periodically tested for STDs.

- Anyone who suspects they have been exposed to an STD should be checked by a physician immediately.

- Most STDs can be treated effectively if diagnosed early.

- STDs are preventable.

- Chlamydia is a curable sexually transmitted infection which is caused by bacteria. Chlamydia can be passed on during oral, vaginal or anal sexual contact with an infected partner. If left untreated, it can cause serious problems in men, women and newborn babies of infected mothers. Nearly 4 million people are infected each year.

- Crabs are parasites that live on the pubic hair in the genital area.

- Gonorrhea is a treatable bacterial infection of the penis, vagina or anus that causes pain or a burning feeling as well as a pus-like discharge. Gonorrhea is also called "the clap."

- Hepatitis is an STD that affects the liver.

- Genital warts are a virus that affects the skin in the genital area, as well as a female's cervix.

- Syphilis is a treatable bacterial infection that can spread throughout the body and affect the heart, brain and nerves.

- Vaginitis is caused by different germs including yeast and trichomoniases. It is an infection of the vagina resulting in itching, burning, vaginal discharge and an odd odor.

- Every year there are 15 million new cases of STDs.

- One in four new STD infections occurs in teenagers.

- Two-thirds of all STDs occur in people 25 years of age or younger.

What is AIDS?

AIDS, which stands for Acquired Immune Deficiency Syndrome, is a very serious disease that affects children, teens, and adults. It is caused by a virus called the human immunodeficiency virus (HIV). This virus is **acquired** and causes a **deficiency** in the body's **immune** system. AIDS is rapidly becoming the leading cause of death in young adults and children in many areas in the United States. There is no cure for AIDS, but there is one way to prevent it - educate yourself and your children about AIDS and HIV, including those behaviors that can increase the risk of getting AIDS.

What are HIV and AIDS?

HIV is the virus that causes AIDS. When persons are infected with HIV, it means the virus is attacking their immune system. The immune system is the body's way of fighting infections and helping prevent some types of cancer. Damage to the immune system from HIV can occur over months, as sometimes happens in infants. Sometimes it occurs slowly over years, as more often happens in adults. *AIDS is diagnosed in an HIV-infected person when the immune system is severely damaged or when certain other serious infections or cancers occur.* Many people do not know they are HIV infected because it can take many years for serious symptoms to develop. However, even if they feel well and have no symptoms, they can spread the infection to others.

Many people with HIV infection look and act healthy. You cannot tell just by looking at people whether they are HIV infected. A blood test for HIV is the only way to be sure

149

How is HIV Spread?

HIV is spread from one person to another through certain body fluids. These fluids include blood and blood products, semen (sperm), fluid from the vagina, and breast milk. The following are ways HIV can be spread:

- **By sexual intercourse (vaginal, anal, or oral) with a person who is HIV infected.** Both males and females can spread HIV. Latex condoms can help prevent the spread of HIV and other sexually transmitted diseases (STDs). *The safest course, however, is to abstain from all forms of sexual intercourse until married or in a long-term mature relationship with an unaffected partner.*

- **Through contact with an infected person's blood.** Sharing syringes or needles for drug use or for other activities such as tattooing or ear piercing can spread HIV. Accidental injuries from contaminated needles can also cause HIV infection. This can happen if a person comes into contact with used needles that have been thrown away. Rarely, HIV has been spread by an infected person's blood directly through the mucous membranes, cuts, scrapes, or open sores of another person.

- **To a baby by his or her HIV-infected mother.** This can happen during pregnancy, labor, delivery, or breast feeding.

- **Through blood or blood products from blood transfusions, organ transplants, or artificial insemination.** This occurs very rarely because donors of blood, tissues, and organs in the United States are tested routinely for HIV. Test results must be negative before the donated fluids and tissues are used.

How is HIV *Not* Spread?

It is very important to know how HIV is **not** spread. Fear and wrong information about HIV and AIDS have caused much suffering to those who have been infected with HIV. Make sure you and your children understand that HIV **cannot** be spread through casual contact with someone who has AIDS or is HIV infected.

You cannot get HIV from:

- *shaking hands*
- *hugging*
- *sitting next to someone*
- *sharing bathrooms*
- *eating food prepared by an HIV-infected person*
- *the air*
- *insect bites*
- *giving blood*
- *swimming pools*

Teaching Your Young Child about HIV and AIDS

Children need to learn about HIV and AIDS at a very early age. By the time your children are 3 or 4 years old, make sure you have clearly explained the following to them:

- They should never touch anyone else's blood or open sores.

- They should never touch needles or syringes.

- If they see someone who is bleeding or if they find a needle or a syringe, they should tell an adult.

- Remind your children never to touch a needle or syringe if they find one in the garbage or on the ground.

150

- AIDS cannot be caught by playing with HIV-infected children.

By grade-school age, your child should begin to have a better understanding of illness and body parts. They should begin to learn more about how HIV can and cannot be spread.

What are the Symptoms of AIDS?

Symptoms of the opportunistic diseases associated with AIDS may include:

- Swelling or hardening of glands located in the throat, groin, or armpit;

- The appearance of hard, discolored or purplish growths on the skin or inside the mouth;

- The appearance of a thick, whitish coating on the tongue or mouth, called "thrush," which may also be accompanied by a sore throat;

- Increasing shortness of breath;

- Periods of continued deep, dry coughing that are not due to other illnesses or to smoking;

- Recurring fevers and/or night sweats;

- Rapid loss of more than 10 pounds of weight that is not due to increased physical exercise or dieting;

- Bruising more easily than normal;

- Unexplained bleeding from growths on the skin, from mucous membranes or from any opening in the body;

- Repeated occurrences of diarrhea.

- Whether or not such symptoms prove to be AIDS related, a doctor should be consulted if any of these symptoms occur.

How Can People Avoid Getting Aids?

To avoid getting aids:

- When having sex, follow "safer sex" guidelines;

- Know your partner's health status and whether or not he or she has other sex partners;

- Do not exchange certain bodily fluids (blood and semen);

- Limit the number of sex partners (preferable to one person who has done the same);

- Use condoms;

- Never share needles to inject drugs (boiling does not guarantee sterility)
- Do not share toothbrushes, razors, or other personal items that could be contaminated with blood;

- Maintain a strong immune system:

    – eat well
    – get enough rest and exercise
    – avoid recreational and illicit drugs
    – avoid heavy use of alcohol
    – have regular medical check-ups

People with HIV are at risk for AIDS and people who carry the AIDS virus must not donate blood, plasma, sperm, body organs or other tissues.

How Do Women Get AIDS?

Like men, women can get AIDS by sharing needles with HIV drug users or by having sexual intercourse involving exchange of bodily fluids with a person who has AIDS or who is infected with the AIDS virus. A few women have developed AIDS following transfusions of contaminated blood.

Any pregnant woman who knows or thinks she may carry the virus should immediately consult a health care provider who is knowledgeable about AIDS, as the AIDS virus is very likely to spread from her to the fetus during pregnancy. It is also important to consult a health care provider if her partner has AIDS, if she or her partner is an HIV drug user or if either is having other sexual relationships.

Is There a Test to Determine if a Person Has Been Exposed to Aids?

Blood tests determining exposure to the AIDS virus are available through private physicians, hospital clinics and blood banks, as well as most local, state and federal health departments. The tests are designed to detect antibodies to AIDS. *The presence of AIDS antibodies in a person's blood means that they have been exposed to the AIDS virus, but does not mean that the person has, or will have, AIDS.* Though they are highly accurate, AIDS antibody tests can only be reliable in detecting infections that are more than four months old.

Who Should be Tested for Antibodies to Aids?

There are several considerations to make before deciding to be tested for antibodies to AIDS:

- Testing positive for AIDS antibodies does not mean that a person has, or will develop, AIDS;

- Test results cannot distinguish persons who have developed an immunity to AIDS from those who have not;

- Positive test results, if leaked to an employer or insurance company, can lead to serious and prejudicial consequences;

- Since there is no medical treatment for a positive result, testing might lead to overwhelming anxiety and psychological distress;

- Birth control pills, alcoholism, and other factors may cause false positive results indicating infection when there is none.

Confidential testing may be appropriate, however, for people at risk for AIDS and/or for their partners who:

- Are considering parenthood;

- Are considering enlistment in the armed forces;

- Have been exclusively monogamous for a number of years and wish to disregard safer sex guidelines.

How is AIDS Treated?

Currently, there are no medicines that can cure AIDS and, for now, there is no vaccine to prevent it. Anonymous testing is available, as well as therapies to treat separately each of the many opportunistic diseases affecting people with AIDS, but these therapies vary in success from one person to another, and none of them is a permanent cure.

It is possible, though, to ease the burdens of this frightening, tragic and often lengthy illness. Many people with AIDS, their families, friends, neighbors and health care workers have made major strides by coming to terms with the feelings of fear, helplessness and inadequacy that surround AIDS. Learning to cope with the overwhelming personal catastrophe of AIDS has also led them to recognize that there are other non-medical elements that are essential in the treatment of people with AIDS.

People with AIDS not only require the most advanced medicines and chemical therapies, they also require psychologically positive environments. *The latest medical research indicates that there is a direct relationship between a person's psychological outlook and the function of his or her immune system.* The ingredients for maintaining the healthy outlook of a person with AIDS are those of any normal and healthy life. They include:

- Companionship;

- Access to places of worship in the community;

- Access to social, educational and recreational facilities

- Access to a job.

Members of the community need to realize that no one has ever contracted AIDS in any way other than those listed previously.

Taken from Planned Parenthood of America and the American Academy of Pediatrics.

Family Home Practice Assignment

1. Review the information on AIDS and HIV with members of your family.

2. Spend a minimum of 30-45 minutes each day playing, reading, and/or massaging your child(ren).

Notes and Comments:

153

Chapter 35

Developing Children's Sexual Self-Worth

Sexual self-worth is the respect children have for their own bodies, gender, sexuality; and the bodies, gender and sexuality of others. Today, the sexual abuse of children and women is at staggering proportions. It is estimated that one out of every four females will be victims of some form of sexual abuse sometime during their lifetime. One in every eight to ten boys will also experience some form of sexual abuse in their lifetime. The numbers indicate something is terribly wrong in the way generations of parents have been preparing their children to handle the responsibilities of sex.

Goal: ***To empower children to own, protect, and respect their sexual being.***

154

For decades, the messages we have sent to children are:

1. You don't need to be concerned about your genitals. They're private. So private we don't touch them, talk about them or even wonder about them. And...

2. If you think about them, we certainly are not going to call them by their biological name. Forget penis and vagina. You now have a winkie or a kitty or a pocket book or a snake or who knows what. And...

3. If you refer to "those places" then you must know that "those places" are dirty and touching them is "bah-bah." And...

4. If anyone is ever going to want to touch you in those dirty snake and kitty places you shouldn't be concerned about, tell them "No!"

How can any child protect something they don't own, don't value and shouldn't think of? If they don't own it, it's doubtful any child can protect it. And yet we wonder why children can't say no to unwanted touch. How can they? We have taken all reasonable skills away from them. The cycle of sexual abuse is clearly one that can be dramatically reduced with proper education. And until the adult community realizes the travesty of the "education," more and more children will fall victims to sexual abuse.

Building Sexual Self-Worth in Children

Imagine your child as an adult, happily in love with their partner, or husband or wife. Imagine your child as a competent, healthy adult, capable of giving and receiving love, capable of enjoying both physical touch and emotional intimacy. If you can dream this dream, you can live this reality. Here's how:

1. **Teach correct body terminology.** Sexual self-worth begins to develop in infancy and continues throughout life. The first step in building positive sexual self-worth is by teaching your children proper sexual body part terminology. Penis, vagina, testicles, buttocks, breasts are commonly accepted terminology. Tubby times, getting dressed or undressed, and putting lotion on are all natural times body part recognition can occur.

2. **Nudity, no big deal.** Make a big deal out of something, and it becomes a big deal. Be casual, it becomes casual. Shame is the biggest barrier in comfortable nudity. Shame teaches something is not right about bodies, nudity or having children see their parents without clothes.

There are natural times that children can see their parents without clothes, like taking a tubby together, or coming out of a shower and getting dressed. During these times, children can learn the difference between being male and female, can view a mature adult body (which can answer many questions they have), can ask questions about being born, being inside mommy, etc. Children can also learn that bodies need to be cared for, cleaned and groomed, and respected. *Nudity is a very natural way of helping children learn to value, protect and care for their body, and the person within.*

155

3. **Honesty is the best policy.** When children seek information about sex, i.e. how babies are made, age-appropriate answers are the best policy. Provide simple responses in a matter-of-fact tone that will satisfy a child's curiosity. The benefit of such discussions is the practice of open and honest communication. During the discussion share your moral views. Example: "Babies are made when two adults who love each other want to bring a child into this world who they can share their love with."

4. **Teach children about touch.** Everyone has a history of touch, and parents create touch history every time they touch their children. There are three kinds of touch:

- **Gentle Touch:** Hugs, pats, handshakes, rubdowns, massages.

- **Hurting Touch:** Slaps, spankings, fights, kicks, bites.

- **Scary Touch:** Touching of sexual body parts (breasts, genitals, buttocks), or the threat of hurting touch (Do you want a spanking?")

When children learn about the different types of touch, they will be better able to recognize and reject unwanted touch.

5. **Respect personal space.** Everyone has an area of personal space immediately surrounding their body. This space is private, restricted space that only those permitted (verbally or non-verbally) can enter. Permission can come in the form of two open arms waiting to give or receive a hug (non-verbal), or a child asking for a hug or a back rub (verbal).

Parents and other adults who regularly violate the personal space of children by zipping an unzipped zipper, or wiping a runny nose, or grabbing a child's hand, or wiping a dirty face without requesting permission, send a message that the child's body is open territory.

Using any type of hurting touch clearly violates the personal space and shows enormous disrespect for a child's body.

6. **Respect a child's right to say no.** Saying "No!" as an expression of disagreement or refusal is an important protective behavior for children. If children are ever going to fully protect themselves from unwanted touch, they must have the right to say "no" to unwanted hugs and kisses from members of their own family.

Building Sexual Self-Worth in Yourself

Children will feel comfortable with their bodies and their sexuality if parents feel comfortable with theirs. To build your sexual self-worth, here are some ideas.

1. **Relax and accept yourself – which includes your body.** In the privacy of your room, stand in front of a full-length mirror naked and admire this wonderful person you see. If you don't like what you see, work on changing it - not rejecting or denying it.

2. **Schedule a time to get a full body massage.** And we're not talking about "massage parlors" either. Rather, a spa that employs licensed massage therapists. An hour and a half with a trained massage therapist can not only serve as a great stress reducer and muscle relaxer, but also as a physical affirmation of the beauty of your body.

156

3. **Take care of your body.** Work out, walk, run, play sports - move it somehow. Watch what you put into it. Too much of anything is not good. That's why they call it "too much."

Mirror, Mirror on the Wall

4. **Finally, increase your self-awareness of the education you received on sexuality.** The Home Practice Assignment presented in this lesson can help begin that process.

Body Parts Exercise

1. What name did you have for your genitals as a child?

_____

_____

_____

_____

_____

2. What name do you have now for your genitals?

_____

_____

_____

_____

3. What name do your children have for their genitals?

_____

_____

_____

_____

4. Identify your biggest fears in teaching your children correct names for their genitals?

_____

_____

_____

_____

_____

157

Family Home Practice Assignment

Answer the following questions with your partner or close friend.

1. What memories do you have of your childhood sexual education?

2. Who were the most instrumental people in teaching you sex education? Was it helpful or hurtful?

3. What are your biggest anxieties about issues related to sex, nudity and body part terminology? Do you know how they originated? Do your anxieties help you or hinder you?

4. On a scale of 1 (low) to 5 (high), rate the following and offer rationale for your rating:

    a. I like my body.
    b. I like the way I look.
    c. I like the person I am.
    d. I feel comfortable discussing sex-related matters with my partner.
    e. I feel comfortable discussing sex-related matters with my children.

5. Make a plan for discussing sex-related issues with your child(ren). If necessary, invite a friend to help out. Remember, keep the discussion factual, honest and relevant to the age of the child.

6. Spend a minimum of 30-45 minutes each day playing, reading, and/or massaging your child(ren).

Chapter 36

Nurturing Bed Time Routine

At some point in almost every child's life, getting ready for bed and going to sleep are two of the least favorite things to do. Much to the heartache of many parents, trying to get children to take naps and to get plenty of sleep often results in a lot of stress and frustration for both the children and the parents. Not surprisingly, in some families, bedtime becomes a battle time, where parents and children both end up stressed out or in tears.

Bedtime is one of the most important times of the day for children. It is a time of rest, relaxation, and rejuvenation for the excitement that awaits them in a new day. Establishing a nurturing routine at bedtime, one in which children feel good about going to sleep and resting, is very important. Before we discuss how to establish a nurturing bedtime routine, let's examine some basic facts and myths about children's sleep and some common bedtime and sleep problems.

Goal: *To increase parents' ability to implement a nurturing bed time routine.*

159

Basic Facts of Children's Sleep

Although different children may have different needs related to sleep, there are some basic facts about children's sleep. Let's review them.

1. Infants are born with irregular sleep cycles which take almost 6 months to mature. Expect your baby to have some difficulty in establishing a consistent pattern of sleep.

2. Newborns sleep an average of 16 to 17 hours per day. However, they may only sleep from 1 to 2 hours at a time to 4 to 5 hours at a time.

3. Babies sleep in stages. The first stage is the **Deep Sleep Stage** where the eyelids are firmly closed and there is little body movement. Children are difficult to awaken in this stage.

The second stage is the **Light Sleep Stage** or the **Slow Waking Up Stage.** Your baby may experience some light whimpers, there might be some irregular breathing, and the baby's eyes appear to be moving under their eyelids. Children are easier to awaken in this stage. If left alone, some children may go back to sleep.

The third stage is the **Awake Stage** where the eyes are open and the baby is responsive to touch and will most likely begin feeding.
As children get older, their need for sleep decreases. Toddlers and preschoolers generally need 10 to 12 hours of sleep each night.

Myths, Wives Tales and Fears

The practices of parenting and child-rearing have for generations been filled with stories, half-truths, myths, old wives tales, and fears. An abundance of these relate to children's sleep and bedtime routines. Let's present some of the more popular ones, and you guess if they're myth or truth. Ready? Let's begin...

1. Keeping a baby up during the day will help him sleep through the night. What do you think? **Myth.** Babies need adequate daytime rest.

Keeping a baby awake all day will only result in an overtired, irritable child who will be less than a pleasure to be with. However, because infants get their days and nights mixed up, try keeping them awake for longer periods of time during the day, and try to avoid the 4 to 5 hour deep sleep occurring late in the afternoon. Ok, let's try another one.

2. A good baby will sleep through the night. Myth or Fact? **Myth again.** All babies are good babies. A baby's worth should never be judged by their behavior. Remember, babies need to develop sleeping patterns. As they continue to develop, so will the length of their night-time sleep develop. But, expect your newborn to awaken during the night and require your help to go back to sleep again.

3. Myth or Fact? If you pick up a crying baby at night, you'll spoil him. Well, there is a little **myth and fact** in this one. Let's explain why.

One of the greatest fears parents have is in spoiling their children. And anyone from grandparents to pediatricians will give you advice on how to and how not to spoil your child. One constant warning is: "Don't pick up a crying child at night. Children will get used to being held, and will demand to be held to fall asleep."

If the only times children are held is when they're crying and in need, or when it's sleep time, they begin to associate being held with these times. And, repeated over time, a pattern will develop and the demand to be held will be viewed as "spoiled behavior." The baby is behaving the way he was taught.

Touch is a basic human need. In babies and young children, it is critical for life itself. Touch and close physical skin-to-skin contact help children's bodies to grow, help them digest their food better, and help the part of their brain responsible for regulating emotions and attachment to grow and flourish. Touch is the equivalent of "Miracle Grow" to help children develop healthy and strong.

To reduce the "spoiling fears of touch," here are some suggestions.

- Hold and touch your baby throughout the day. Use a front carrier. If you need to be reassured this is okay, go to the zoo and watch the way other mammals care for their young. Have you ever heard of a spoiled monkey or kangaroo?

- Incorporate infant massage into your sleep and bedtime routines. Start when your child is a baby and keep massaging right through grade school. Kids love it and so do parents. It's a special bonding time as well as a means of stimulating healthy brain development.

- Play with and talk to your baby when they're awake. There is simply no substitute for good quality time between parent and child to build feelings of trust and security which will help your child develop good bedtime and sleep patterns.

- Ok, here's another one. If you bring your baby to bed with you, you'll never get him out. **It's a myth**. We know what some of you are thinking. "If I let my child sleep in the parent's bed, he'll be there well into his 30's. You'll never get him out." Well, rest assured. They do get out.

The family bed has been used for generations in cultures throughout the world. Bed sharing, especially if breast feeding at night, is perfectly okay. Research suggests bed sharing is safe and may even reduce the chance of crib death as long as the parents don't drink alcohol in excess and pass out or take sleeping pills. However, young children also need to learn to sleep in their own beds. So use a crib for daytime naps.

- How about this one: To prevent night waking, let children cry themselves to sleep. Myth or Fact? **Myth**, of course. Children who cry themselves to sleep do so out of sheer exhaustion. And, the longer the child cries, the more panicky he becomes, the more stressful the

161

parents get. The only time it is ever advisable to let a child be left crying in a crib is if the parent feels she might hurt her baby. Ten to 15 minutes away from the baby to calm down, reduce your stress, and get it back together will help you respond in a nurturing way to your child.

- Last one: The goal of attending to a crying baby is to get him to stop crying as soon as possible. **Myth**. The goal is to comfort a crying baby, not necessarily to stop him from crying. While it's true the two often go together, children who are comforted generally stop crying. A parent's patience may wear thin if stopping the crying is her primary and immediate goal. Children cry for a variety of reasons, which include being hungry, stressed, overly tired, frightened, sick, or colicky. By approaching your crying child with the goal of stopping the crying, the child is expected to comply with the parent's demand. When the child doesn't respond, parental stress increases which may result in injury to the child. By approaching your crying child with the intent of comforting your child, realizing full well this may take some time, the expectations remain with the parent, not the child.

General Guidelines for Helping Children Develop Good Sleep Habits

Here are some general guidelines to help children develop good sleep habits.

1. Keep the room temperature at a comfortable degree. A temperature between 65 and 68 degrees is often comfortable.

   The current recommendation for baby's sleep position is to place the baby on their back or side, never on their stomach. Infant sleep deaths have been linked to babies sleeping on their stomachs.

2. Avoid putting your baby to bed with a pacifier. She may wake up without it and begin to cry. Pacifiers are used to satisfy the baby's need to suck, not to help them sleep.

3. For toddlers and preschoolers, make sure there is a quiet time period before bedtime.

4. Dress children in bed clothes that do not restrict their movement.

5. Allow toddlers and preschoolers to sleep with safe objects that help provide them with a sense of security. Stuffed animals and blankets are good comfort objects.

6. Often a little background noise is helpful and reassuring to the child in helping a child fall asleep. Total silence may be too scary.

7. A gentle night light avoids the need to turn on a main light and can offer a sense of security for children.

8. While it's not always possible, try putting babies to bed at the first signs of drowsiness rather than when they are completely

162

asleep. It's ideally best to let baby learn to relax himself to sleep.

9. And lastly, establish a nurturing bedtime routine and make it a consistent part of their day.

Building a Nurturing Bedtime Routine

To make bedtime a more pleasant experience, the following ten steps are suggested.

1. **The first step in establishing a nurturing bedtime routine is identifying a consistent time your child will be going to bed.** Inconsistent bedtime only creates confusion which ultimately leads to resentment. Identify a bed time and be consistent.

2. **Make a nice relaxing bath time part of the nighttime routine for going to bed.** A nurturing bath time routine will serve as a positive preview for what's to come in getting ready for bed.

3. **Dress your child in clothes especially for bedtime.** Getting dressed in pajamas and sleepers is an indication that it's getting close to bedtime. If you can get fun bedtime clothes with pictures of animals, or cars, or cartoon characters, etc. on them, getting dressed for bed will be even more fun.

4. **Help the child get dressed for sleep in their bedroom, not in other rooms of the house.** Keep the association between bed, sleep, and bedtime clothes. As a parenting practice, praise gives children positive feedback to increase their feelings of competence and confidence in themselves and their behavior.

5. **Have your child brush their teeth every night as part of the bedtime routine.** What an excellent habit to develop at a young age. Model the way to brush teeth by

brushing your own. Giving your child their own toothbrush to play with and use is strongly recommended as part of the bedtime routine.

6. **Spend time with your child reading stories.** Find a cozy rocking chair, have your child crawl up on your lap, get snuggled in, and read for awhile.

7. **Choose bedtime books that are happy and pleasing – books which add comfort, not discomfort.** Save the scary stories for daytime reading when the child gets older. By the way, you might want to negotiate with your child how many stories you are going to read.

8. **When finished reading, tell your child it's time to lie down in bed.** Putting your child in the bed before he is asleep is recommended. Some children who fall asleep in their parent's arms wake up during the night and wonder where mommy and daddy went. Getting into bed before he is

asleep serves to get the child used to falling asleep alone. Then, nighttime awakenings aren't as scary.

9. **Tuck your child in and tell your child a power story.** A power story is a recap of all the wonderful things your child did or tried to do. Name the story after your child: "This is Alicia's power story." Make sure you tell them the wonderful things they did that day, or how much you love them as a person. Give them a hug or kiss and wish them good dreams. If you can, sing a song or two. A parents' voice can be reassuring and can help your child relax and get cozy.

10. **If your child should begin to cry during the night, go into his room, and find out what the problem is.** Remember, crying is a signal of distress. The child is asking for help. Find out what he needs. A little reassuring is often all that is needed for him to fall back asleep.

Bedtime and Sleep Problems and Solutions

Babies who wake up from sleep crying whether in the middle of the night or in the middle of the afternoon are clearly experiencing some discomfort. Discomfort can be classified into two categories: Physical and Emotional.

Some areas of physical discomfort include:

- Hunger
- A gassy stomach
- A wet or soiled diaper
- Being restricted from moving by their clothing, or
- Sickness and fever

The remedies to these problems are related to their cause. A dad with a bottle or a mom ready to nurse is the baby's version of fast food. A burp, clean diaper and less restrictive sleeper usually gets baby back to sleep. And, if you believe in divine intervention, the middle of the night would be a good time to ask for a little help from your maker. It couldn't hurt! If baby still can't settle down and he continues to cry, he may be sick. Check to see if baby is feverish. He may have an ear infection, or may be allergic to his formula. In any case, call a doctor or nurse. Many health care clinics have 24-hour help lines. Make sure you keep this number available to you at all times.

Sometimes toddlers and preschoolers have difficulty going to bed or staying asleep because of emotional reasons. Some areas of emotional discomfort include:

- Scary dreams, commonly called nightmares

- Stress and anxiety related to fighting between parents.

- A death in the family.

- Siblings not getting along.

- Problems at school or with a teacher.

- Community violence and crime.

- Weather conditions.

- TV programs they're watching, or video games they're playing.

- The bedtime stories being read. Are they contributing to his discomfort?

- Bedtime that is too early. Everybody else is staying up and having a good time.

164

In any case, parents need to be understanding and reassuring. A child who feels the respect of his parents will be better able to understand and work through his fears. And remember, this too shall pass.

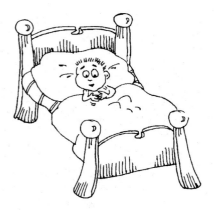

Things That Parents Should Never Do

1. Never, ever, ever shake or throw your baby. No matter how angry, frustrated, or stressed out you get, shaking and throwing your child will cause permanent physical injury or death.

2. Never leave your child asleep in the house alone, or in the care of their brother or sister who is too young to be a resource in case of an emergency.

3. Never tell a child his bedtime fears are ridiculous and there is no need to be frightened. Honor your child's fears and respect their need to be comforted and reassured.

4. Never put your baby to bed with a propped-up bottle. Your baby could choke.

5. Once again, never lay your baby down on his stomach to sleep. Stomach lying is for toddlers who are practicing strengthening their neck muscles with their parents or other adults watching.

6. Do not use your child's bedroom as a place of punishment. Bedrooms that are also used as places of punishment provide little comfort at night as places of security.

7. Establishing a nurturing bed time routine for your children is clearly one of the most challenging parts of being a parent of a baby, toddler, and preschooler. Handling your child's sleep problems may be difficult and it is normal to become upset when a child keeps you awake at night. Stay committed to helping your child develop better sleep habits. Don't be embarrassed to ask for help and support, and don't forget to find times to nurture yourself. You deserve it.

References: Sleep Problems in Children. American Academy of Pediatrics. 1994.

Family Home Practice Assignment

1. Practice implementing the Nurturing Bed Time Routine with each of your children.

2. Continue practicing other nurturing routines for feeding, diapering and dressing, and bath times.

3. Spend a minimum of 30-45 minutes each day playing, reading, and/or massaging your child(ren).

Notes and Comments:

Chapter 37

Handling Stress

Goal: *To increase parents' ability to recognize and handle stress.*

What is Stress?

Stress is an emotional response to the demands of life. It is the pressure we feel to meet a deadline, to keep a schedule, to expect others to keep their commitments or to raise caring children in a seemingly hostile world. Stress is the one feeling most everyone is concerned about, and for good reason. *It is estimated that 75 - 90% of all illnesses are stress related.* Getting a handle on stress can, for a lot of us, mean a healthier and longer life.

Good Stress and Bad Stress

Not all stress is bad. Actually, there is some stress that's good. Stress is a normal part of life. When our life has purpose and we have dreams we want fulfilled, the challenges of fulfilling these dreams creates stress, but the kind of stress that energizes us.

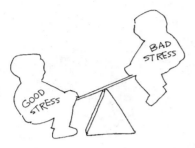

Good stress activates us to use our personal power in positive ways to meet our needs, desires, and wants. The kind of stress that is bad is called *distress*, or stress that drains us physically, emotionally, and socially. Bad stress or distress shows up in signs like headaches, backaches, ulcers, diarrhea, fatigue, anxiety, depression, lashing out, withdrawing from others. Chronic distress can result in severe illnesses like colitis, cardiac problems, stroke and cancer.

Distress and Unmet Needs

Distress can often be attributed to our inability to get our basic needs met. As previously mentioned, getting our basic needs met is the functional purpose of our behavior. Getting our needs met reduces our stress, allows us to be the caring parent we want to be, and allows us to help our children get their needs met and, in turn, reduces their stress. Nurturing our selves as men and women is a great way of reducing our stress.

Handling Stress

The most important aspect of stress is the ability to handle it. Since most stress is self-induced, the ability to handle it rests primarily with each person.

The following are some strategies that are proven in reducing stress.

Physical Approaches

- **Get regular exercise.** Exercise increases our strength and stamina. Try exercising with a friend. You can get your social needs met by being with your buddy and your emotional need met for fun and support.

- **Improve your diet.** Stress and diet are closely linked. We all know what we should eat, yet don't take too seriously the practice of eating healthy meals. Balance is the key.

- **Listen to your body.** Minimize the wear and tear on your body by listening to its messages (stiff neck, headaches, etc.) Massages, rub-downs, and hot baths are great stress reducers.

167

- **Learn relaxation skills.** There are many simple relaxation techniques, however, none are effective unless they are used. Visualizations are great to use when you're holding a crying baby in the middle of the night, hoping the child will stop so you can go back to sleep. When you feel less stress, so will your child who will then proceed to fall asleep.

- **Get adequate sleep.** Get six to eight hours sleep per night, or if night sleep is not always possible, take naps during the day.

Mental Approaches

- **Adopt a new attitude.** Try to be less rigid, less perfectionist, less competitive, and less impatient. Flexibility is a key stress reducer.

- **Increase self-worth.** Replace negative self labels ("I'm no good!") with positive self labels ("I can succeed!").

- **Set realistic expectations.** Review all the "shoulds" and "musts" in life and deter- mine which are worth keeping and which are worth getting rid of.

- **Keep a positive outlook.** Get rid of the prejudices, the negative labels of others, and the view of the world as negative. A positive outlook does wonders for reducing stress.

- **Improve your communication skills.** Use problem solving, negotiation and compromise; don't keep things inside, share your feelings; listen to others and learn from others.

- **Leave work at work.** People need to get away from work and leave it behind. Bringing your work home with you is a sure way to stress out yourself and your family.
- **Get organized.** Make a list of things that need to get done, evaluate what's really important, and value free time.

Social Approaches

- **Develop a support network.** Friends are important to share good times and bad. Don't close down, stay open.

- **Develop a social life.** People with a strong peer network who are active socially live longer and happier lives. Be active, meet others, and join social clubs.

- **Volunteer your time.** Helping others is a good way to reduce stress. By reaching out and helping others, we empower ourselves as well as those we're helping.

- **A sense of humor.** Humor is one of the first things that goes when people are stressed out. Laughter is the voice of children. Be child like. Play and find the lighter side to issues.

- **Relax.** Recreate, meditate, be alone and contemplate life, go for nature walks, read.

- **Develop hobbies.** Train collecting, bird watching, stamp/coin collecting, shop flea markets, cultivate a garden, plant trees. Develop outside interests and invest your time and energy.

Family Home Practice Assignment

1. Identify five stressors (things that cause stress) in your life.

   a. _____

   b. _____

   c. _____

   d. _____

   e. _____

2. Make a plan how you can reduce or prevent these stressors from dictating the quality of your life.

   _____

   _____

   _____

   _____

3. Develop a plan to cope with the stressors you can't change.

   _____

   _____

   _____

   _____

4. Identify five stressors (things that cause stress) in your children's lives.

   a. _____

   b. _____

   c. _____

   d. _____

   e. _____

5. What can you do to help your children reduce their stress?

   _____

   _____

   _____

   _____

6. Spend a minimum of 30-45 minutes each day playing, reading, and/or massaging your child(ren).

Chapter 38

Helping Children Manage Their Behavior

Goal: *To increase parents' ability to empower children to manage their own behavior.*

There are more behavior management techniques that foster children's healthy growth and development available than most parents could ever expect to use. But remember, a technique is only as good as the way it's used. When parents complain a technique is not working, it's obvious it's either the wrong technique, or a misuse of the right technique.

Following are some helpful techniques that you can add to your bundle of techniques already presented. These are some of our favorites my wife and I use with our three children. These are techniques proven to help children grow up healthy and caring. They're fun to use and they accomplish their goal.

170

Giving Children Choices

To help children utilize their power in a positive way, give them choices to make decisions on issues they view as important. Children will feel more powerful and use their power in a positive way because choices:

- Provide opportunities for children to use their power.

- Help children learn to manage their own behavior.

- Let children know they have power.

- Is a good way to defuse potential power struggles.

- Help children take responsibility for their behavior.

Giving children choices can begin early in a child's life. The following are some areas where choices can be given:

- **Dressing:** "Son, what shirt would you like to wear, your blue one or your green one?"

- **Eating:** "Amy, would you like to drink your milk in a red cup or in a white cup?"

- **Bath Time**: "Carson, do you want to play first and then take a bath, or take a bath first?"

- **Play Time:** "Tommy, do you want to ride your bike or play with your trains?"

Choices and Consequences

Providing children with choices for their behavior and consequences for those choices is another excellent technique in helping children manage their own behavior. When using Choices and Consequences, first share the options children have, and then the consequences for each of those options.

Some examples:

- "Children, you have a choice. If you continue to argue over the toys, both of you will lose the privilege of playing with them. If you share them and take turns like I expect, you can continue playing."

- "Rachel, I expect you to use good table manners to eat your dinner at the table. If you continue to act silly, you will have to leave the table. It's your choice."

Some important points to remember when using Choices and Consequences:

- **Never use threats as choices.** Example - "If you don't leave your sister alone, I'm gonna break your neck." Parents either can't carry the threats through or don't want to.

- **Never give ultimatums as choices.** Example - "I'll never talk to you again if you don't shut up!" Ultimatums can rarely be carried through and soon children will learn your words are hot air.

CAUTION!!! *Never give choices when there aren't any.* Example - "Son, would you like to get your coat on now? We have to go!" If the child answers, "No," but he really has to get is coat on anyway, he never really had a choice. Never give a choice when you cannot accept "No" as an answer.

Remember: Consequences must be related to the behavior you wish to increase or decrease.

Using Humor

Without a doubt, happy children are easier to be with, manage and encourage than children who are angry, resentful and oppositional. Humor is an outstanding strategy to help children learn to manage their own behavior, as well as an effective way to prevent arguments, rebellious behavior, and power struggles.

Did you know that by using humor you also help your child develop their sense of humor? Children begin to develop a sense of humor when they're very young. In fact, some researchers claim that a child's sense of humor develops before they begin talking. The game, "Peek-a-Boo" is a good example. Children laugh and laugh when a face appears. And it is well known that laughter and a sense of humor are great ways to relieve stress.

The following techniques demonstrate when humor can be put to use in parenting children:

- **Fooler Approach.** Ever try to fool someone? Well, this can be a great way to get children to do things they're supposed to do. The first step in the fooler approach is education. Teach your child what it is you want. Give them an example:

   "Christie, when I say I want you to set the table, I need you to put the plates, cups, and silverware on the table like this." (Demonstrate what you want).

   The second step is to give them a non-example. This is where the fooler approach comes in: "But, I bet I can fool you. When I say, 'Christie, please set the table,' I expect the table to be set like this' (give a non-

example - silverware in the cups, or plates turned upside down, etc.) "Is this what I want?" The child will obviously say, "Nooo Daddy! This is what you want," and she goes about doing it the right way.

The fooler approach is a fun way to teach and get cooperation. It's also a great stress reducer.

- **Reverse Psychology.** Another technique to help children accomplish a task is reverse psychology. *The object is to say exactly what you don't want, but mean exactly what you do want.* A father attempting to get children to the supper table says, "All right, food is on the table, but I don't want any of you here watching television to come join us. You guys stay right there." The children, knowing it's a game, race to the table ahead of Dad.

- **Talking Objects.** Talking bathtubs, ice cream bars, shoes, etc. are all helpful in getting children to cooperate. A shoe that says, "Put me on, put me on!" is much more exciting than a parent telling a child, "Put on your shoes." A bathtub calling a child to jump in is more fun than a parent telling a child to get in the bathtub.

- **Transition Time.** Providing children with a transition time between activities and before requests is important. No one likes to be told that they have to do something immediately. Mentioning to children, "Five more minutes and it will be time to eat," helps children prepare to make the transition from what they are doing to what you want them to do.

- **Asking "What can you do instead?"** So many times parents are asked to solve a problem or to remedy a situation. While we parents certainly give our two cents worth, a better way would be to empower your children to come up with their own solutions. "Well sweetie, what can you do instead?" Encourage several solutions and both of you pick out the best one or two. If you're stuck on which one to do, identify the positives and the negatives to each solution. The one with the most positives is generally the better solution.

- **Asking "What have you learned?"** Making mistakes is one thing - learning from them is another. Asking, "What have you learned?" from both success and failures is a powerful way to empower children with insights. Let them tell you and sit back in amazement.

Notes and Comments:

Family Home Practice Assignment

1. Select one or two of the behavior encouragement techniques and try them out. Later in the week, try the other one. Note the successes you have with each approach.

_____

_____

_____

_____

_____

_____

_____

_____

_____

_____

_____

_____

2. Praise your children for being and doing.

3. Spend a minimum of 30-45 minutes each day playing, reading, and/or massaging your child(ren).

173

Chapter 39

Ignoring as a Parenting Technique

Goal: *To increase parents' ability to ignore irritating, unwanted behavior of children.*

Ignoring is a form of behavior management used to reduce or eliminate behaviors of children parents find especially irritating. Ignoring is a way parents communicate their disapproval of certain behaviors by deliberately not paying attention in words or actions to undesirable behaviors whenever they occur. Not paying attention means absolutely no acknowledgment in any manner that the behavior is present.

174

What Ignoring is Not

Ignoring is not threatening, hitting, or criticizing children because of some undesirable behavior. To criticize a behavior, parents have to pay attention to it. To some children, any kind of attention, even negative attention, is reinforcing.

By paying attention to the undesirable behavior, parents are actually encouraging children to continue to perform the behavior.

When and What to Ignore

Praise what you want to see more of; ignore what you don't want to see more of. Three rules for behaviors that you should never ignore:

1. **Harm to Oneself or Others.** Any hurtful behavior to oneself or to others should not be ignored. Some examples include harm to pets, hitting other children, saying mean things to others or to oneself, hitting oneself or pulling one's own hair. These need immediate intervention.

2. **Degree of Potential Harm.** Any behavior that increases the risk of physical harm to the child or other children cannot be ignored. Playing with matches or inserting objects into an electrical outlet are examples of two behaviors that cannot be ignored.

3. **Damage to Property.** Behaviors that damage or destroy property should not be ignored. Writing with spray paint on an interior or exterior wall, stepping on plants, or breaking toys are behaviors that require immediate action.

Before You Use Ignoring

1. Decide what behavior you want to see instead. Mention to the child you're ready to see it and that nothing would be finer than the child performing that desirable behavior.

2. Be sure you can tolerate the behavior without eventually giving in or punishing the child.

3. Decide whether you can tolerate the behavior without having to remove the child from the area.

4. Realize that you will have to ignore the behavior 100% of the time, no matter how long it lasts.

5. Try redirecting the child to another activity or getting their interest in some other topic. Sometimes, kids, like anybody, get stuck in a pattern of behavior. And with a little help, they can move on to more appropriate behavior.

175

6. Try to be predictive. If you know your child is tired and is less likely to participate in a family event, get a babysitter. A little preventive planning can make for an enjoyable evening.

How to Ignore

1. Discuss with your child how irritating certain behaviors can be. List these behaviors in your Family Rules, making sure you also list the wanted, desirable behaviors.

2. When the behavior occurs, give the child one reminder, referring to the family rules.

3. Ignoring means absolutely no attention. Do not look at or talk to the child. Any attention, even threats and criticism, will reinforce the behavior. Focus your attention elsewhere. Dream your favorite day dream, plan your fantasy vacation, or relive a happy memory.

4. The behavior may continue for one minute, ten minutes, or 30 minutes. Ignore the entire time. The behavior may turn for the worse before it gets better. If that happens, don't give in, even though you may feel angry or embarrassed.

5. When the behavior stops, praise the child immediately, "I'm sure glad you stopped your temper tantrum. I don't like temper tantrums, and it's much nicer to be with you when you aren't screaming." This is the good consequence. The child has now learned a temper tantrum did not get your attention, but when they stopped, you gave your attention.

6. If anyone else is reinforcing the inappropriate behavior, like a sympathetic grandparent, brother, or sister, you will have to convince them to ignore the behavior also.

7. ***When using ignoring as a technique in changing behavior, you do not ignore the child, you ignore the irritating behavior.*** The child soon gets the message that even though you love them, you do not like the undesirable behavior.

Family Home Practice Assignment

1. Practice using Ignoring as a behavior management technique. Keep note of the times it works successfully and the times it doesn't.

2. Make sure you teach your children what are appropriate and inappropriate ways to ask for things, excuse yourself, interrupt, etc. Tell them about ignoring and how you are going to handle unwanted behavior.

3. Spend a minimum of 30-45 minutes each day playing, reading, and/or massaging your child(ren).

Notes and Comments:

Chapter 40

Toilet Training

Goal: *To increase parents' ability to practice nurturing ways to toilet train children.*

Teaching children to use the toilet is not as difficult as perhaps you are imagining. With careful planning and the right conditions, children can learn to use the toilet in a matter of a few days to a few weeks. But before you start to teach your child how to use the toilet, there are many important things that must be checked first.

Is Your Child Ready?

Age
A good general rule to follow is that children should be at least 2 years old before you begin potty training. Generally, potty training happens for children between 18 months and 4 years of age.

Gender
Boys generally take longer to be potty trained than girls.

Muscle Control
Can your child walk yet? Can he put little objects into bigger objects? Can your child pull their pants up and down? Does he have good muscle control? If he doesn't he won't be able to control his bladder or his bowels. Physical coordination is necessary before you begin toilet teaching.

Physical Development
The maturity of the bladder is also important to consider. A couple of indicators that suggest your child's bladder capacity is ready for toilet training are: a dry diaper after napping, and a steady flow of urine rather than several episodes of dribbles.

Communication
Your child will need to be able to communicate his intentions to urinate or have a bowel movement before he can be taught to successfully use the potty. He has to be able to make some sound or make some facial expression or physical movement to let you know he has to go. If he cannot communicate his intentions, he's not ready to learn to use the potty.

Follow Verbal Instructions
Your child will have to be able to follow instructions before you can start successful toilet teaching. Simply, if a child can't follow verbal directions, when you tell him to "hurry and go use the potty," he may be thinking you are talking some foreign language. Give your child verbal instructions and see if he can follow through. If he can't, successful toilet teaching will not be accomplished.

Desire
Lastly, before you begin toilet teaching, you have to determine whether or not your child has the desire to learn. All the other preconditions listed will serve little value if your child simply refuses to use the potty. Desire to use the potty will speed up the learning process greatly.

Before You Begin Your Teaching

The following suggestions will help you prepare your child to use the potty.

1. **Words to Use.** Parents need to help children decide on words to use to indicate that the child needs to either urinate or have a bowel movement. Use any words you like, but it helps if the words make sense so others can understand about your child's needs when you're not around. Some words parents use are silly, confusing, and eventually embarrassing. Words like tinkle, shimkle, udo, shoo-shoo, wee wee, tee, tee, #1 or #2, kaka, or BM all mean the child has to urinate or have a bowel movement. The words the child will use depend a great deal on the preference of the parents. Keep the words simple so a child can say them, yet they are understandable enough for others.

2. **Model the Appropriate Behavior.** Let the child see you and other family members using the bathroom. When you go, you can say, "Mommy (Daddy) is going pee pee in the toilet." That way, your daughter or son notices how adults use the toilet. The same sex parent as the child is generally preferable. Children may become confused watching opposite sex family members urinate. If you're a bit embarrassed by the thought of your child watching you go to the bathroom, ask an older son or daughter. Older siblings generally don't mind going to the bathroom with their younger brother or sister around.

3. **Buy a Potty Chair.** Before you begin teaching your child how to use the toilet, it's a great idea to first purchase a potty chair. Purchasing a potty chair encourages your child to see it, play with it, and become familiar with it before he begins to use it.

The separate unit potty chair, the one that stands on the floor, is generally considered better than the unit that attaches to the toilet. The separate standing unit allows the child to place their feet on the floor which adds to feelings of security and comfort.

Let the child examine the potty, play with it, take it apart, carry it around, before he begins to use it. Again, the more comfortable the child is with the potty, the greater the chance that they will want to use it.

4. **Buy Training Pants.** Your child will need to wear training pants instead of diapers when you begin toilet teaching. Help him learn to pull them up and pull them down. Fancy-looking training pants with pictures of your child's favorite singer, or cartoon character, might make it just a bit more enjoyable to wear training pants. If your child is still in diapers, do not attempt to start toilet training. There will be just too much frustration in getting the diaper off in time to use the potty.

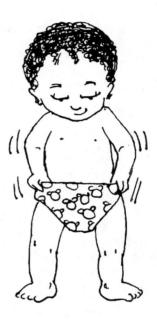

Starting the Training

When you decide your child is ready to learn how to use the potty, try to pick a good day to begin.

It will probably help both you and your child to begin the task of learning to use the toilet if both of you are in good moods. A cranky child, or one who has had a bad night's sleep, can make the task of toilet teaching very frustrating. In this situation, the parents who desire to teach the child may also become frustrated and unknowingly non-supportive and even punitive. Teaching your child to use the potty should be fun, not confrontive.

Plan to set aside the entire day for helping and supporting your child. Make the task of introducing the potty your only task for the day.

Teaching Potty Training

1. Try to make a realistic guess when your child will likely need to use the potty. After lunch, before nap, after nap, after breakfast? Becoming aware helps you to be available and pay extra special notice to possible potty times.

2. When you notice your child is about to urinate or have a bowel movement, guide him to the potty and help him pull down his pants.

3. Talk to your child. Use the words you decided on for urination and bowel movement. Say to your child, "Adam is about ready to make poo-poo in his potty. Oh, what an exciting time!"

4. Stay with your child in the bathroom while he is having a bowel movement. Keep him company, read a story or two.

5. Praise his efforts. It might take some children awhile to do their bowel movement. Don't pressure your child, support him.

6. When he is finished, praise your child. Don't be afraid to let him know how proud you are of his efforts, not of him. Children are anxious to get their parents' attention and approval. Don't be stingy with your praise.

7. Teach your child how to wipe himself. Girls should always be taught to wipe themselves from front to back. It's a good habit to start early, one that will help prevent bladder infections in the future. Teach boys to shake off the drips before getting their pants back on.

8. Teach boys and girls to wash their hands after using the toilet to practice good hygiene.

9. After your child has gone in the potty, you can empty the potty in several ways:

   - You can empty the potty in the toilet and flush the toilet while your child watches.

   - Your child can help you empty the potty, perhaps by flushing the toilet.

   - You can empty the potty after your child has left the room.

Some children are very sensitive and may become upset that a product of their body is disappearing. Consequently, you may not want to flush the toilet until they leave the room. Some children are less worried about that issue and may want to take an active role in discarding the potty material. Be sensitive to your child's needs and act accordingly.

Accidents Will Happen

Expect that your child will have accidents in the beginning. Accidents are a normal occurrence. When an accident happens, talk to your child and reassure him. "Oh Oh. Adam made poo poo in his pants. Too bad. Next time Adam will do poo poo in the potty. Let's change your pants. Poo poo in your pants probably doesn't feel very good." *The main thing to remember when accidents happen is: Don't make a big deal about them. Make a big deal when your child uses the potty successfully.*

Copyright 2009   Family Development Resources, Inc.   www.nurturingparenting.com   1-800-688-5822

If your child misses the potty and wets or soils the floor, reassuringly tell him, "Oh Adam missed the potty this time. Can you put your pee pee (poo poo) in the potty next time? Thanks for trying son!" *Always encourage your child to use the potty.*

If your child begins to act as if he never heard of, let alone used a potty, remain supportive and talk to your child. Several things may be going on that could be contributing to your child's regressing:

- The child feels less attention is being paid to him.

- A new brother or sister in the family has taken over the spotlight.

- Too much pressure is being put on using the potty correctly.

- Family problems, separations, divorces, extended absences, moving to a new home, illness, etc.

- If your child continues to wet and soil himself, put him back in diapers. This way, the pressure is lessened for you and for him.

Some Final Points to Remember

- **Never, ever use punishment in teaching your child to use the potty.** Punitive, abusive practices only cause increased anxiety and can lead to very severe problems. The point that punishment is harmful in teaching children to use the potty cannot be stressed enough.

- **Once your child has begun to use the potty, keep the potty in the bathroom.** Don't get into the habit of moving the potty in front of the TV to amuse your child. You don't move your toilet in front of the TV, so don't move the potty. The bathroom is the place where toilets and potties belong.

The greatest single outcome that a child can learn from the whole experience of toilet teaching is positive regard for himself or herself as a boy or girl. Keep this fact in mind as you're helping your child learn to use the potty.

Family Home Practice Assignment

1. If appropriate, practice potty training your child with techniques and steps presented in this chapter.

2. Take time to nurture yourself.

3. Spend a minimum of 30-45 minutes each day playing, reading, and/or massaging your child(ren).

Notes and Comments:

Chapter 41

Understanding and Expressing Your Anger

Anger is an Emotion

Anger cannot take over anyone unless they allow it to. Anger is not a gun, it is not a fist fight, it is not domestic violence, or anything else portrayed in the movies or in the news. Anger is only an emotion, one in which given proper understanding and education, can be controlled.

Feelings or emotions can be placed into two categories: feelings of comfort and feelings of discomfort. Anger is a feeling of discomfort. The goal of any emotion is to be expressed. It needs to come out. If it doesn't, it builds up like a volcano and explodes. This is as true for feelings of discomfort as it is with feelings of comfort.

Goal: *To increase parents' ability to express anger in appropriate ways.*

182

All feelings exist on a continuum. Let's take the number range of 0 to 10 with 0 being the complete absence of anger and 10 being the highest form of anger or rage.

Stages of Anger

None	Mild	Moderate	Severe	Rage
0	1 2 3	4 5 6	7 8 9	10
Blue Zone		**Orange Zone**	**Red Zone**	

1. All feelings have energy. That's the way they get expressed. Also, it's the energy that needs expression.

2. The goal in expressing anger is to catch the feeling early so it doesn't build up inside. In the early stages of anger (1, 2, 3 or the Blue Zone), mild discussions can occur in which a person can share their anger with a great deal of control. People are still pretty cool and very much in control.

3. As the feeling of anger increases into the Orange Zone (4, 5, 6 or the Orange Zone), mild discussions move into more "heated" discussions as voices get louder, adrenaline increases, heart beat increases, blood is flowing more rapidly, words become distinct and pronounced, jaws get tighter and the intensity has picked up a great deal.

4. When anger gets into the Red Zone (7, 8, 9), a person has less logical control and the feeling of anger is overtaking judgment. This is the zone when discussions turn to abuse, name calling, screaming, yelling, and fighting. Threats, physical assault, and beatings are all Red Zone behaviors.

5. When anger reaches rage (10), people are typically out of control. In rage, anything goes - which is usually someone's life.

Where Does Anger Come From?

Anger is a secondary emotion. By that we mean, anger is the result of hurt not being expressed. *The longer hurt stays inside, when hurt gets a chance to be expressed, it comes out as anger.* And depending on how much past hurt there is, the anger can come out as mild, moderate or severe.

Anger and Violence

Anger does not have to be released in violence, but it often is. This is likely the result of watching more models of anger equals violence than models of anger equals non-violence. Don't believe us! Turn on the TV and watch any program. Anger expressed as violence is constantly there. Coupled with the additional models of parents fighting when angry, sports heroes fighting, talk show guests fighting, etc., it's easy to understand why people get violent when they get angry.

Perhaps the biggest reason why anger gets expressed as violence is the education young children get, primarily boys, in hitting something.

Parents unknowingly teach the association between anger and violence every time they tell their children to hit something as a way of releasing their anger energy. Hitting some<u>thing</u> quickly translates into hitting some<u>one</u>.

Violence is a learned expression of anger, and because it's learned it can be unlearned. It's not easy re-learning a new way to express anger, but it can be done.

Anger Management Plan

To keep anger from dominating or destroying your life and the lives of those around you, here are some suggestions:

1. **Find non-violent ways to release pent up anger energy.** Be creative. Come up with some physical way to exert your energy so you can remain in control of your anger. Jogging, exercise, basketball or other sports, writing, or cleaning the house are some ideas. Come up with others that are good for you.

2. **Express your emotional hurt or pain when you feel it.** Do not store it up inside. Usually saving things is a good idea. Not so with pain. Talk to a caring friend, relative or professional. Let it go and be free.

3. **Avoid situations or people that push your button.** If you are aware of things that can simulate anger in you, try to avoid those situations or people. Avoid them until you're sure that you can remain in control and not be influenced so strongly that you lose it. Or, if they're such a powerful negative force in your life, find a way to lessen your involvement with them.

4. **Make a pledge to yourself and others around you that you will give up getting violent when you're expressing your anger.** While you are destroying things and people around you, you are probably also destroying your life. Think about it.

5. **Drinking, or getting loaded or blasted are not ways that will ultimately serve you well in managing your anger.** If they work at all, they do so temporarily. When you're sober again, the anger monster is still there.

6. **And finally, embrace your anger, don't disown it.** To accept something is to acknowledge it exists and that you are responsible for your actions.

To own your anger is to acknowledge that you certainly are capable of getting angry and making a mess of things by hitting,

yelling, rejecting others, and generally being a big pain in the butt to be around. *When you own your anger, you can control it and then you can work on changing how you behave.*

Notes and Comments:

Family Home Practice Assignment

Make a plan to control your anger, and be able to express it in the way you desire. Complete the following:

1. Three things in my life that I get angry with are:

    a. _____

    b. _____

    c. _____

2. List the ways you express your anger in each situation:

    a. _____

    b. _____

    c. _____

3. List three things you can do to avoid getting angry in the situations listed in #1 or things you can do to change the situations that would result in preventing your angry response:

    a. _____

    b. _____

    c. _____

4. List three ways you would like to express your anger:

    a. _____

    b. _____

    c. _____

5. Identify things you feel keep you from expressing your anger in the ways you identified in #4:

    a. _____

    b. _____

    c. _____

6. With this awareness at hand, make a plan to appropriately express your anger or to change the situations that promote your anger. You may want to involve other family members in this plan and write it down.

    a. _____

    b. _____

    c. _____

7. Spend a minimum of 30 to 45 minutes each day playing, reading, and/or massaging your child(ren).

Chapter 42

Helping Your Children Express Their Anger

Goal: *To teach children healthy ways to recognize and express their anger.*

Don't Get Angry at Me - I'm Your Father!

Wrong! Wrong! Wrong! If your children can't get angry with you, how are they going to learn how to express their anger appropriately? The home is the in-service workshop for the outside world. If kids can't practice expressing emotions at home, when they go into the outside world they will be ill-prepared. And, many parents get calls or visits from school or community officials with the explanation that their child responded to a situation at school in a way that was deemed by the authority figure in charge to be highly inappropriate. In other words, your kid punched out another kid on the playground because he was being teased, or for any one of the thousands of reasons kids have.

And so the kid gets home and you give him a two-hour lecture and top the whole thing off with a spanking and the threat of future violence as a punishment if this kind of behavior continues. So what to do to straighten out this mess? Read on.

The Right to Get Angry

Here are some principles of anger management. Please indicate whether you agree or disagree with each one by circling Agree or Disagree:

1. The goal is to teach children how to express their anger appropriately rather than telling them not to get anger.

    Agree?   Disagree?

2. It's OK for children to get angry with other family members.

    Agree?   Disagree?

3. Teaching children to hit a pillow to let off their steam is a bad idea.

    Agree?   Disagree?

4. Children learn how to express anger by observing others express their anger.

    Agree?   Disagree?

5. Hitting children teaches them to hit others.

    Agree?   Disagree?

If you agree with each of the items, we're on the same wave length. If you disagree with one or more of the items, let us explain.

1. The goal of parenting is to teach skills, values, and morals. Handling anger is a skill. Expressing anger in a non-violent way is following the family's moral code. Watching parents express their anger in a non-violent way is following the family's values. Watching parents express their anger non-violently supports the "value of the family morals (right and wrong ways of doing things.) So, when you get angry, model how to express anger appropriately.

2. The home is the primary learning place for children. Home is where children learn to practice what they are being taught by their parents. *However, being angry with other family members does not mean lack of respect.* Hitting, spitting, name calling, swearing - these are all disrespectful ways of expressing anger. In Nurturing Parenting,

respecting yourself, others and the environment is a principle held highly. Anger is okay. Disrespectful ways of expressing anger are not.

3. It is a bad idea to teach children to hit a pillow when they're angry. By telling children to hit anything when they're angry teaches them to pair the emotion of anger with the behavior of hitting. Plus, it can be a very scary practice. Ever see people get angry in restaurants and pound the table, or get angry in their car and ram another car? Ever see kids fight because they were angry? Ever see athletes fight during a game when they got angry? Ever see a tennis player pound their racket on the net, a golfer pound their club on the ground, or a football player pound his helmet on the turf? Ever see or hear of a man pound on his wife because he got angry? Ever feel another person pound on you when they got angry?? Ever pound on or want to pound on your child when he or she "made" you angry? The practice of hitting associated with the emotion of anger is not a good skill to teach children.

4. In spite of our willingness to accept this fact, children are not violent by nature. They learn how to be violent through observing others and through direct experience. Aggression is a human trait. Violence is

learned. Take an emotion called anger, mix in the human trait of aggression and add in learned violence, and the phone calls, referrals, and rough times will be the norm. Start educating by modeling different ways to express anger, by responding to your child in a non-violent way, and problem solving the mess the kid is in, and you have a great chance to turn things around.

5. Hitting children does teach children how to hit others. Research and clinical studies have, for decades, proven this point. Yet there are parents and a small minority of professionals who still refuse to accept this fact. Their response is what we call denial. Let's you and me face reality and stop this nonsense of violence.

Teaching Children to Express Anger

This step-by-step plan is designed to be implemented at home with all family members - not just the kids. If it's good for the goslings (young geese) it's good for the goose (mom goose) and the gander (dad goose). So gooses, listen up.

Step 1 Talk with your children about anger.

- It's the expression of past hurt that wasn't expressed.

- When children feel hurt or pain or loss, talking about it is good. Keeping it inside is not.

- Tears are a good way to express pain and hurt. If kids can't cry because they're "not supposed to" or if the "boys don't cry" attitude exists in the house, time for a major

shift in attitude. If boys can't cry, hurt, feel loss, pain, etc. and are taught to keep the feelings inside you have the foundation for anger. The more hurt and pain inside, the more anger is ready to come out.

Step 2 Emotions are feelings that have energy that need expression.

- Sometimes mild anger energy can be released through talking about it.

- When moderate or severe levels of anger exist, it's better to release the energy first, then talk second.

Step 3 Anger is okay; it's the way it's expressed that needs work.

- This is where anger management comes in. Everyone needs a plan in what behavior is acceptable and what is not. Some guidelines we recommend:

Respect yourself; don't hurt yourself.
Respect others; don't hurt others.
Respect your environment; don't destroy property or nature.

Step 4 Expressing anger occurs in two stages: release of energy, and talking about what led up to the anger.

- Sometimes mild anger energy can be released through talking about it.

- When moderate or severe levels of anger exist, it's better to release the energy first, then talk second.

188

Step 5   Brainstorm ways to release the energy.

- Keep in mind the suggestions stated in Step 3.

- Identify two or three things that your child can do to release their energy. Remember, the "I can hit something" suggestion and explain why.

- Some suggestions for anger energy release: any exercise or active sport, dancing to loud music, drawing, any activity like cleaning the house, vacuuming the floors, etc.

Step 6   Talk about what happened that led to the anger. Talking is a way of connecting the feeling of anger with its logical cause. This connection is an important one.

Step 7   Make a plan and reward efforts.

A Last Thought: Angry Kids Hurt Animals

Kids who purposefully hurt animals are in need of help - big time. *Hurting animals is not a phase kids go through. It's a sign of a child in trouble!* There is too much research evidence that parallels the abuse of animals with other destructive and potentially life-threatening behaviors. Hurting animals is serious and children who abuse animals need counseling. Observe how pets are treated in your home. Having pets is a terrific way to build empathy, teach caring, and build responsibility. Remember: abuse is the opposite of caring, and violence is the opposite of empathy. Treat pets with respect and help build empathy in your children.

My Child's Anger Management Plan

Five ways I want my children to be able to express their anger are:

1. _____

   _____

2. _____

   _____

3. _____

   _____

4. _____

   _____

5. _____

   _____

Family Home Practice Assignment

1. Carry out the seven-step process presented in Helping Children Learn How To Express Their Anger.

2. Spend a minimum of 30-45 minutes each day playing, reading, and/or massaging your child(ren).

Notes and Comments:

189

Chapter 43

Communicating Thoughts and Feelings

It's What You Say and How You Say It!

"Sticks and stones may break my bones but words can never hurt me!" Wanna bet? If words can never harm us, why does just about everyone get upset when they're criticized, poked fun at, talked harshly to, and yelled at. What is said does hurt, and the way words are said also hurts. You can tear down the self-worth of a child through constant criticism and blame. It's called verbal abuse, and it destroys many lives.

Goal: ***To increase parents' ability to use communication as a behavior encouragement technique.***

The key to healthy communication is to communicate your thoughts and feelings to your children in a manner that does not purposefully hurt them, or encourage them to think less of themselves. Healthy communication is by far one of the most difficult skills of nurturing parenting. Since we talk all the time to our children, healthy communication requires constant monitoring. But still, there are things that get in our way. Let's look at a few of them.

Blame "You make me _____"

You should know you're in trouble when you begin any communication with "You make me …" Two reasons:

- "You make me" is blaming.
- "You make me" is powerless.

Blaming children for the way the parents feel is one of the cardinal sins of parenting. Why? First, it shows parents have less power and children have more power in determining how and what parents can feel. When parents give up their control of how they feel, children gain an enormous amount of power. Power, I might add, that they don't want. They have enough trouble handling their own feelings let alone the responsibility for handling their parents' feelings.

Secondly, blaming demonstrates incompetence. The message sent is "I can't handle my feelings so I'll blame you." Blaming is an act of the incompetent.

- **"You make me feel so angry."**
- **"He made me feel upset."**
- **"She made me feel sad."**

Most kids are probably thinking, "If I could make you anything, I'd make you be quiet."

Blaming = Incompetence

The reality is we are responsible for the way we feel in the same manner we're responsible for our personal hygiene. Nobody makes us stink. People stink because they don't use deodorant and wash daily. *Taking responsibility for our feelings is no different than taking responsibility for our personal hygiene.*

Taking Responsibility for our Feelings

Thomas Gordon, a pioneer in parenting education, came up with a method for taking responsibility for communicating feelings without blaming others. He calls it: I Statements, You Messages.

I Statements are expressions about me. These expressions can focus on how I feel, what I need, or about what I think.

For example, I Statements about how I feel may be: "I feel angry;" " I feel excited;" or, " I feel depressed." I statements about what I need may be: "I need a hug;" I need some quiet time."

I Statements about what I think could be: "I think I will not go;" " I think I am lost;" or "I think the team should trade for a good quarterback." I Statements make you the center of attention, the star of the moment. *I Statements focus on you, tell about you, and describe you.*

You Messages are about someone else. They are your perceptions of how someone else feels, about what someone else needs, or about what someone else thinks.

191

Some examples of You Messages regarding someone else's feelings could be: "You look angry;" "You seem excited;" or, "You appear depressed."

You Messages regarding someone else's needs could be: "You need a hug;" "You need a glass of water;" or, "You need some quiet time."

You Messages regarding someone's thoughts could be: "What do you think about nuclear energy?" "Do you think the team should trade for a good quarterback?"

You Messages make someone else the center of attention, the star of the moment.

You Messages focus on someone else, tell about someone else, or describe someone else. The big difference is that messages about someone else are only guesses or perceptions about how they look, how they feel, or what they need. Only that person knows for sure if the You Messages are accurate.

Ownership of Feelings

The main difference between I Statements and You Messages centers on ownership. When used appropriately, I Statements convey ownership of feelings, thoughts and needs. Each person is responsible for their own feelings.

That is, no one can make you feel, think, or need something you don't want to. Although others can influence your decision, the final say belongs to you and no one else. When people use I Statements, they are taking ownership of what they feel, think, or need. Taking ownership of your own feelings, thoughts, and needs is the first step in using I Statements appropriately.

You Messages cannot express ownership of feelings simply because no one can own anyone else's feelings, thoughts, and needs. Ownership belongs to the person.

Appropriate and Inappropriate Use of I Statements

The use of I Statements is appropriate when a person wants to send some message about themselves. Such statements convey ownership and represent a clear statement of the person's feelings, thoughts, and needs.

- "I am angry because the room is not clean."
- "I am not aware of any restaurant open this time of night."
- "I need to spend some time by myself in order to unwind."

I Statements are often used inappropriately. Sometimes people use I Statements in order to manipulate others into doing something. Some examples of the inappropriate use of I Statements may be:

- "I'm so upset at what you're doing that I might have a heart attack."
- "If you don't do it my way, I will get a migraine headache."

These statements are manipulative. Their intent is to control someone's behavior. The clear message and the ownership of the feeling is not present.

Appropriate Use of You Messages

You Messages are used appropriately in five ways:

1. **To give choices.** You Messages work well in combination with choices and consequences: a message is being sent to the child. The message describes alternative plans of behavior and their expected consequences.

   An example may be: "Carson, you have a choice. You can clean your room now, or you can clean your room later. However, if your room is not cleaned by 6:00 p.m., you can't watch TV tonight. It's your choice."

In this instance Carson was the center of attention. As you already know, giving children choices helps them develop a sense of responsibility.

2. **To give praise.** You Messages work well when praising; the center of attention naturally belongs to someone else. That's the time for a whole string of You Messages.

- "You must feel very proud."
- "You did that so well!"
- "I bet you feel really good."

Letting someone know how proud you are would be a good use of You Messages, as long as the center of attention remains with the other person.

3. **To gain clarification.** You Messages are ideal to send when you desire clarification. As mentioned earlier, You Messages are your perceptions or guesses about how another person feels, what another person is thinking, or what another person needs. When a You Message requests clarification, we are essentially asking for validation. Are my perceptions right or wrong? Some examples are:

- "You seem to be really angry."
- "You don't seem to like the movie."
- "You appear sad."

The receiver is able to respond to the question(s) based on a quick inventory of how he's feeling. Sending a You Message for clarification helps the sender know the state of being of the receiver. It also lets the receiver know how he appears to be acting.

4. **To ask questions.** Asking questions is a very natural and appropriate way of using You Messages.

- "Are you hungry?"

5. **To reflect feelings.** Reflecting feelings gives children a chance to identify how they might be feeling, or an awareness that they know you're aware of their feelings.

- "Darlinda, you seem to be feeling very sad."

Inappropriate Use of You Messages

No one likes to have feelings of discomfort. It doesn't feel good to be angry, sad, afraid, depressed, or out of control. All people have these feelings at some time or another during their lives. ***When we have these feelings of discomfort, it's often difficult to take full responsibility for the feelings.*** It's easier and much safer to blame someone else for the way we feel. In that way, we don't have to take responsibility for our actions.

Statements like: "You made me angry," "You made me lose control" are good examples of You Messages that are blaming. They are the adult version of the child's "He made me do it."

Increasing Family Communication

The appropriate use of I Statements and You Messages is important for establishing and enhancing communication among family members. The ability to accept and receive praise, to carry out nurturing behavior encouragement and management strategies, to listen to the needs, feelings, and thoughts of children, and to communicate feelings, thoughts, and needs all center around your success at using I Statements and You Messages. ***The time and energy you invest in learning how to send I Statements and You Messages will pay rich dividends.*** They will increase honest communication between you, your children, your partner, and friends.

The Formula for Communicating with "I Statements"

The following formula is presented as a guide to help us take responsibility for our feelings. Remember the four conditions and enjoy healthy communication.

I feel _____

(State a feeling)

when _____

(Describe the exact behavior)

because _____.

(State the need that relates to that feeling and any thought or belief related to it)

What I want is _____.

(Describe the exact behavior that would meet the need)

Examples:

"I feel happy when toys are picked up, because I need to have things tidy in order to feel good about our house. I want to thank you for being so considerate of my need for order."

"I feel very disappointed when your brother is hit because one of our family rules is no hitting. What I want and expect is cooperation in following the family rules and for you to use another way to express your anger."

Helpful Hints:

1. Take time to think it through before you confront.

2. Use a sincere voice that expresses caring.

3. Be concrete and use specific examples.

4. Make eye contact when appropriate.

Family Home Practice Assignment

1. Practice honoring children's desires. Notice the effect.

2. Help your children make a plan to express their feeling energy in constructive ways.

3. Model appropriate ways to express feelings.

4. Spend a minimum of 30-45 minutes each day playing, reading, and/or massaging your child(ren).

Notes and Comments:

194

Chapter 44

Criticism, Confrontation and Rules for Fair Fighting

Goal: *To improve parents' communication skills.*

Criticism and Confrontation

Essentially we have two choices when we have to tell another person something about them that needs improvement. Choice #1 is to say what we have to say to the other person without regard for the other person's feelings. This style is often referred to as criticism. The other choice, Choice #2 is to say what we have to say to the other person with regard for the other person's feelings. This style is referred to as confrontation. Confrontation is different from criticism in style, approach and intent

195

Criticism: It Hurts So Bad!

What's wrong with criticizing others? Here are five good reasons for choosing a different style of communicating your dissatisfaction.

- **Criticism hurts.** It's supposed to hurt. It's like slapping someone in the face with the mean words. It's verbal abuse.

- **Criticism destroys.** Criticism never feels good to the person being criticized because criticism tears people down. *Constructive criticism is a term made up by people who criticize a lot just to feel good about their own mean words.* Constructive criticism is a lot like a "good slap in the face."

- **Criticism blames.** No one likes to be blamed for something they did or didn't do, regardless of the person's age. Blaming never tells people the right things to do. It only focuses on the bad, always!

- **Criticism closes people up.** People become defensive. They often begin to act like a mummy. They do nothing, say nothing, and eventually hear nothing. At least not what you're saying. Teenagers especially tune out when parents are being critical. Who could blame them for tuning out criticism?

- **Criticism creates anger in others.** Some people respond to criticism by getting angry and start to fight back. Criticism is the common ground of all arguments.

Generally, people criticize others out of their own feelings of inadequacy. When you need to knock someone down verbally, most often they are standing emotionally taller than you. It is often said that what we dislike in others is what we dislike most about ourselves.

Confrontation: It Feels So Good!

Confrontation is a process by which you tell your child (or anyone else) how you feel, or what you need, or want or observe, without tearing them down. This is often very difficult because of the intensity that can grip emotions at that moment. Being in control of our emotions and words is the only way confrontation can work.

To confront others is to let them know your thoughts and feelings in a way that communicates respect for them as people. It does not tear down. Confrontation builds self-respect and gives people information. Here are some reasons why confrontation works better than criticism:

- **Confrontation communicates respect for the other person.** When you confront someone on some issue, you are actually comparing your views with someone else's views.

- **Confrontation helps people listen.** When you have an awkward or painful message to share, confrontation keeps people listening. Criticism shuts people down. You have a better chance of others hearing your message when you use confrontation.

- **Confrontation provides useful information.** People can do something with the information they receive from confrontation. Criticism usually tells people what they have not done.

196

- **Confrontation generally promotes a friendship.** True friends confront each other on issues. They are sensitive to the feelings of each other.

- **Confrontation promotes change.** Because people do not have to waste valuable energy being defensive and angry, they can go about the business of doing something about what they are being confronted on.

- **Confrontation is always based out of respect.** People who use confrontation rather than criticism are generally more caring, nurturing and happier people.

Examples of Criticism and Confrontation

Just like you can praise people for whom they are (being) and their behavior (doing), you can also criticize and confront others for being and doing. Let's take some examples:

Criticism
"You're just a lazy slob. Look at this messy room. What are you, some kind of pig?"

Confrontation
"The room needs to be cleaned and I'm disappointed you haven't cooperated and followed our family rules."

****

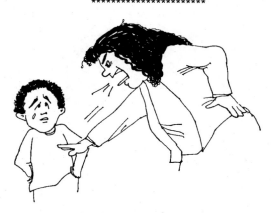

Criticism
"Look what you did! You're gonna regret the day you were born?

Confrontation
"It looks to me like you made a poor choice. Hitting your brother is never OK. You will sit in time-out for 10 minutes"

Criticism
"Your breath stinks like a dead animal! What did you eat - a skunk?"

Confrontation
"Your breath needs some mouth wash."

****

Criticism
"Look at you! You look like a tramp with all that make-up on and that crazy hairdo!"

Confrontation
"I think the amount of make-up you're wearing hides your real beauty. Maybe you can..."

****

Criticism
"Don't stay out late; don't let the guy try anything funny; and don't drink and drive."

Confrontation
"I expect you will be home by curfew. I also know that you will be careful and safe and use good common sense. Have a good time."

But, Can't Two People Argue?

Sure they can! Arguing is a good way for people to express their displeasure, to disagree on a course of action, or for two people to "clear the air" of past hurts and disappointments. But, you guessed it, there are some guidelines we'd like to offer so the argument or "heated discussion" does not get out of hand and flare up into a full-fledged war.

1. **Decide upon a time limit before you begin and STICK TO IT.** No more than 30 minutes, better if it is 15 or 20 minutes. If you don't finish in the amount of time allotted, schedule another time later that day.

197

2. **Decide how many "zaps" you'll permit before you (or the other person) walk out.** A zap is a hurtful remark, an insult, a threat, a sarcastic dig, etc. If a person feels he or she has been zapped, he or she has been. Any attempt to threaten, shame, or blame is another zap. When you get to the number agreed upon ahead of time, walk out.

3. **Choose one problem per session.** Have a session every day for awhile if you need it, but stick to one problem per session.

4. **Try to stay in the present.** It is helpful to stay in the relative present rather than bring up things that happened 12 years ago.

5. **Stick to the point.** Don't get carried away with other problems. One problem per session, stay in the present, and stick to the point.

6. **Own your own feelings.** Avoid blaming your partner for your feelings - they are not anyone else's, they are yours.

7. **Listen to the other person.** You need to hear the other person's point of view to find an agreement for both of you.

8. **Agree upon a solution which is good for both of you**, not just one or the other of you.

9. **Try not to argue at night or in bed.** Night time is for rest; beds are for resting and quiet personal time. If you need to argue, get out of bed, go into the kitchen, sit at the table and argue.

10. **Don't save up issues.** Keep a constant dialogue going between you and your children and partner. Things that aren't spoken but thought and felt will only come back to haunt you and everyone around you. Share yourself with your family. It's a great experience.

Notes and Comments:

Family Home Practice Assignment

1. Write down the model of "arguing" that you observed and experienced during your childhood.

   _____

   _____

   _____

   _____

2. Do you think now that the model was good or not? Why?

   _____

   _____

   _____

   _____

3. What did you learn that you're trying to change or improve?

   _____

   _____

   _____

   _____

4. Practice using confrontation and not criticism. What did you experience?

   _____

   _____

   _____

   _____

5. Spend a minimum of 30-45 minutes each day playing, reading, and/or massaging your child(ren).

Chapter 45

Understanding Alcohol Use and Abuse

Goal: *To improve parents' awareness of the reasons why people drink and abuse alcohol.*

This One's for You

Did you know that alcohol and other drug use and abuse problems cost society in pain, suffering and in dollars? Sure you do. You know the problems: automobile crashes, physical and sexual child abuse, child neglect, rape, assault, vandalism, spouse battering and a host of many other crimes all associated with the use and abuse of drugs - primarily alcohol.

Alcohol is one of the oldest drugs in use and is the most common. The term "alcohol" is a chemical term that covers a class of substances only a few of which are ever consumed. There is isopropyl alcohol used in rubbing alcohol; methyl alcohol or wood alcohol; and ethyl alcohol, used in alcoholic drinks. Alcohol is so widespread that there are few cultures in the world where alcohol is not consumed.

Fruit of the Vine

The origin of alcoholic beverages is lost in the myths of pre-history - which means we can only guess how it all got started. Alcohol involves fermentation which is a process where fruits, left exposed in a warm atmosphere, begin to change. The airborne yeast acts on the sugar in the fruit, converting it to alcohol and carbon dioxide. It is assumed that alcohol was probably discovered accidentally.

Early people probably liked the taste and effect and figured out how to make alcohol. Throw in a few Budweiser commercials and you have as good an explanation as you can find on how alcohol came to be the most common drug used today. There is no mistaking the popularity of alcohol.

It is often the central beverage at births, initiations, marriages, feasts, crownings, worships, hospitality, war making, peace making and funerals. Alcohol has been regulated, prohibited, commercialized and promoted. It is a contributor to many events from tragic to grand. So what makes this beverage so popular?

Happy Hour

It is generally recognized that people drink for two reasons: to feel pleasure and to escape pain. In reality, a drink or two helps many people feel better, at least for a little while. After the drink wears off, whatever was a problem more than likely is still a problem.

Ready for Take-off!

Many people are like ticking time bombs ready to go off at a moment's notice. Suppressed past pain and hurt is expressed as anger. Consequently, people who are angry are also people who have a lot of bottled up pain ready to come out. The pain is bottled up because of their inability or unwillingness to discuss their pain and hurt when it happened. Also, as children, many of us have witnessed or experienced violence in family situations where parents have been angry. So, the stage is set for violence to be expressed given the right conditions.

For many, the right conditions entail alcohol since drinking will help them escape their pain and hurt and momentarily feel better. Serving as a disinhibitor, the alcohol now releases the past pain, which comes out as anger, coupled with the violence they've seen modeled or experienced.

Clearly not all people who drink get violent. Some get sad, flirtatious, happy, withdrawn - the whole range of emotions. They key here is, drinking and the release of feelings are a sure thing.

One for My Baby, and One More for the Road

Never, never, never, never drink when you're pregnant, think you're pregnant, or hoping to get pregnant.

Why Do People Abuse Alcohol?

There are a number of common reasons why people abuse alcohol:

1. **Parental history of problem drinking.** Children of alcoholics are at a higher risk for developing alcoholism than are children in the general population. If both parents are alcoholic, the risk of becoming an alcoholic is probably over 50%.

201

2. **Heavy drinking or drug use.** Clearly, the more a person consumes, the more the body tolerates the alcohol and becomes dependent upon it. Heavy and continuous drinking is a predictable contributor to the increase in alcoholism.

3. **Genetic factors.** More than hair, eyes, and skin color are passed down from parent to child. Research now indicates that the risk to become alcoholic is also passed down from parents to child. Studies of alcoholic family members show that alcoholism runs in families. And, because our society places an importance on alcohol, children from alcoholic families are clearly a risk for becoming alcoholic in their own right.

4. **Psychological problems.** Stress, pressures, problems, suppressed pain all increase the likelihood that a person would use alcohol to help numb these pains. This is especially true for families with a history of problem drinkers.

5. **Enabling.** Enablers are people who make excuses for the problem drinker, or try to cover up the problem or keep it a secret. In many ways, enablers are part of the alcoholic's problem because they shield the alcoholic from all the problems caused by their drinking.

The Effects of Alcohol on Your Body

- *Alcohol is a depressant, and like many other depressants, it acts as a sedative and induces sleep.* Drinking can slow down reaction time by about 10%, has a detrimental effect on memory, vision and judgment, and during periods of heavy drinking, can cause blackouts -- which

makes drinking and driving a foolish thing to do.

- Drinking also encourages many people to become disinhibited. That is, people will do things under the influence of alcohol that they normally wouldn't do when sober. Heavy drinkers are often malnourished because of low food intake and poor absorption of nutrients by the body. Too much alcohol may cause cirrhosis of the liver, inflammation of the pancreas, damage to the brain and heart, and increase risk for many cancers.

- Some studies have suggested that moderate drinking is linked to a lower risk for heart attacks. However, drinking is also linked to a higher risk for high blood pressure and hemorrhagic stroke.

Some People Should Not Drink Alcoholic Beverages

- **Women who are pregnant or trying to conceive.** As mentioned earlier, birth defects have been attributed to drinking by the mother when pregnant. Women who are pregnant, or trying to conceive, should not drink alcoholic beverages.

- **Individuals who plan to drive or engage in other activities that require attention or skill.** Most people retain some alcohol in the blood three to five hours after even moderate drinking.

- **Individuals using medicines, even over-the-counter kinds.** Alcohol may affect the benefits or toxicity of medicines. Also, some medicines may increase blood alcohol levels or increase alcohol's adverse effect on the brain.

202

- **Individuals who cannot keep their drinking moderate.** This is a special concern for recovering alcoholics and people whose family members have alcohol problems.

- **Children and adolescents.** Use of alcoholic beverages by children and adolescents involve risks to health and other serious problems, and it is against the law.

If You Drink Alcoholic Beverages, Do So in Moderation

Alcoholic beverages supply calories, but little or no nutrients. Drinking them has no health benefit, is linked with many health problems, is the cause of many accidents, and can lead to addiction. If adults elect to drink alcoholic beverages, they should consume them in moderate amounts.

If you drink alcoholic beverages, do so in moderation; and don't drink and drive.

What's Moderate Drinking?

Women: No more than one drink per day.
Men: No more than two drinks per day.

Count as a drink:

- 12 ounces of regular beer
- 5 ounces of wine
- 1 ½ ounces of distilled spirits.

Family Home Practice Assignment

1. Complete the Families and Alcohol Use Questionnaire. Discuss your responses with your partner or a friend. Self-awareness is the first step in changing habits.

2. Spend a minimum of 30-45 minutes each day playing, reading, and/or massaging your child(ren).

Notes and Comments:

203

Families and Alcohol Use Questionnaire

About YOU

The following questions are designed to increase your awareness about your alcohol use. Try to answer the questions as honestly as you can.

		Yes	No
1.	Do you feel you have a drinking problem?	_____	_____
2.	Do you often drink to feel better?	_____	_____
3.	Do you often drink to "get through the day?"	_____	_____
4.	Do you spend more money on alcohol than you plan?	_____	_____
5.	Do you feel annoyed or irritated if your family or friends discuss your drinking?	_____	_____
6.	Have you had any arguments with your family or friends because of your drinking?	_____	_____
7.	Have you ever failed to keep a promise you made to yourself about cutting down on your drinking?	_____	_____
8.	Do you tend to drink alcohol at times when you feel angry, disappointed, depressed, anxious, or lonely?	_____	_____
9.	Have you ever been careless of your family's welfare when you've been drinking (driving under the influence, falling asleep with a burning cigarette, not caring where your kids were, blowing a paycheck on alcohol, hitting a family member when under the influence)?	_____	_____
10.	Do you drink in the morning to help you recover from the night before?	_____	_____

About YOUR FAMILY

The following questions are designed to increase your awareness about the alcohol use of any family members. Try to answer the questions as honestly as you can.

1.	Do you feel a member of your family has a drinking problem?	_____	_____
2.	Do you lie awake worrying about your family member (of whatever age)?	_____	_____
3.	Do you feel frustrated in your attempts to control your family member?	_____	_____
4.	Do you argue with your family member about his or her use of alcohol?	_____	_____
5.	Do you find it increasingly difficult to communicate with your family member?	_____	_____
6.	Do you find yourself lying or covering up for your family member?	_____	_____
7.	Do you feel resentful or hostile toward your family member?	_____	_____
8.	Do you worry about your family member's behavior affecting other members of the family?	_____	_____
9.	Has the family member been confronted about their behavior?	_____	_____
10.	Has the family member denied their drinking problem?	_____	_____

Chapter 46

Keeping Children Drug Free

Goal: To increase parents' skills in keeping their children drug-free.

Keeping children drug free is not an impossible task. Millions of children world-wide go drug free. So, what's the secret? Well, by now you should know that there is no secret to raising healthy children. It's hard work but well worth it. Here's our 12-step program for keeping children drug free.

205

Step 1 **Demonstrate caring.** When you care about someone, you act on their behalf.

Step 2 **Show interest.** Ask your kids when they come home how their day was. Help them with or review their homework. Attend school plays and gatherings. Be a presence in your child's school. If your child's teacher does not know your name when you meet - you're not a presence.

Step 3 **Parent without violence.** Forget the good spankings and beatings and tongue lashings. How about some good old' fashioned kindness and respect.

Step 4 **Talk about drugs.** Talk WITH your child, not TO your child about drugs. Talking WITH someone is a discussion/conversation. Talking TO someone is a lecture/speech. The first one is interactive; the second one is boring.

Want to put your kids to sleep? Start preaching to them about the evils of anything. They'll be asleep in the blink-of-an-eye.

Step 5 **Model appropriate drinking.** If you're going to drink alcohol, don't sneak it or only drink when the kids are asleep. They'll know you're sneaking. Model appropriate drinking in front of the children. When they ask what you're drinking, tell them, "Alcohol. Should children ever drink alcohol?" They'll answer, "No!" You say, "Why?" They'll say, "Because it's not good for you." And you say, "What else?" and they'll say, "Because it's against the law." And you say, "And don't you ever forget these facts." And they'll say, "We won't!"

Step 6 **No drinking means NO DRINKING..** *If you want your kids to have a drug-free childhood, then don't you be the one to offer them alcohol.* Some families have "traditions" and rites of passage where at certain ceremonies it's OK to drink, or it's OK to try smoking "just once." If you don't want you kids to steal things, why would you say, "It's OK so steal just this once. It's grandma's birthday and she would like a new radio?"

Step 7 **No Illegal Drugs.** If parents are doing illegal drugs, what chance to you think your kids will have to stay drug free? Slim chance. Anyway, it's against the law, and your miserable life becomes a miserable mess.

Step 8 **Don't compromise your values.** Many parents believe their kids are going to drink anyway, so they would rather have them drink at home. That's just plain dumb. If you believe this, volunteer one night a week at your community drug center and see if you still believe this after one month. Stick to your values.

Step 9 **Just Say Yes to Health!** The problem with being a kid is adults keep telling you to say "No" to this, and "No" to that. Say No, Say No, Say No! As if saying "No" were the answer to preventing all of life's

206

problems. "No" won't work without a "Yes." A kids has to say "Yes" to something else if he's going to say "No." The absence of something is nothing. So, how can anyone do nothing? If they're not doing it, they wouldn't know, and neither would you. If "No" is to drugs - what's "Yes" to?

Step10 **Communicate.** To communicate is to talk and listen. Try listening more and talking less. I bet you'll learn things about your kids you've not heard before.

Step 11 **Have Fun as a Family.** Do things together. Sports, parks, picnics, movies, hikes, dinner, family get-togethers, parties. You name it – then do it as a family. Without alcohol!

Step 12 **Know Your Kids' Friends.** Birds of a feather flock together. Find out who your children hang around with. Let your home be the gathering spot.

Notes and Comments:

| Family Home Practice Assignment |

Discuss the information presented in this lesson as a family. Complete the following exercise:

1. Circle the number that best indicates how you would rate your skills in each step.

Step 1 **Demonstrate Caring**

Very Bad	Bad	SoSo	Good	Very Good
1	2	3	4	5

Step 2 **Show Interest**

Very Bad	Bad	SoSo	Good	Very Good
1	2	3	4	5

Step 3 **Parent Without Violence**

Very Bad	Bad	SoSo	Good	Very Good
1	2	3	4	5

Step 4 **Talk About Drugs**

Very Bad	Bad	SoSo	Good	Very Good
1	2	3	4	5

Step 5 **Model Appropriate Drinking**

Very Bad	Bad	SoSo	Good	Very Good
1	2	3	4	5

Step 6 **Sticking to "No Drinking" Rule**

Very Bad	Bad	SoSo	Good	Very Good
1	2	3	4	5

Step 7 **Not Using Illegal Drugs**

Very Bad	Bad	SoSo	Good	Very Good
1	2	3	4	5

Step 8 **Sticking to Your Values**

Very Bad	Bad	SoSo	Good	Very Good
1	2	3	4	5

Step 9 **Just Say "Yes" to Health**

Very Bad	Bad	SoSo	Good	Very Good
1	2	3	4	5

Step 10 **Communicate with Your Children.**

Very Bad	Bad	SoSo	Good	Very Good
1	2	3	4	5

Step 11 **Have Fun as a Family**

Very Bad	Bad	SoSo	Good	Very Good
1	2	3	4	5

Step 12 **Know Your Kids' Friends**

Very Bad	Bad	SoSo	Good	Very Good
1	2	3	4	5

2. Look at the areas you rate high and the areas you rate low. Do you want to make any changes? Now's the time! A drug-free childhood is a great gift.

3. Spend a minimum of 30-45 minutes each day playing, reading, and/or massaging your child(ren).

Chapter 47

How to Protect
Our Children

The basic philosophy of safety is that children have the right to be safe. Here are some tips for keeping your children safe.

Safety from PHYSICAL Harm

Safety from EMOTIONAL Harm

Safety from SEXUAL Harm

Keeping Your Children Supervised

Goal: ***To increase parents' skills in keeping their children drug-free.***

208

Safety from PHYSICAL HARM addresses many areas:

Safety at HOME

Is your home child proofed?

- Are dangerous objects out of reach? Are small items like paper clips, rubber bands, pop tops from cans, tooth picks, safety pins, picked up off the floor and out of reach of children?

- Are heavy objects away from the edge of tables?

- Can children climb on chairs and get to dangerous objects?

- Is the cat litter box and pet food stored in out-of-the-way locations?

- Are electric sockets capped?

- Do your cabinets have safety locks?

A good thing to do to make sure your home is safe is to crawl around on the floor. What you see and can reach is what your child can see and reach!

Safety in CARS

- Always use a **car safety seat**. Start with your baby's first ride home from the hospital.

- Always use car safety seats for children until they get big enough to sit in the back seat strapped in.

- Never place a child in a rear facing car seat in the front seat. The **air bags** can injure your child.

- The safest place for children to ride is the **back seat**.

- Set a good example and wear your **seat belt**.

- **Never leave your child unattended** in a car with the windows rolled up and the car running or parked.

Safety with BABY SITTERS

Children are subjected to a variety of people who are charged with their temporary care. Baby sitters are the most frequently utilized to care for children followed by family members, and families of friends that children know from school, church, and after school activities.

Knowing whom you are leaving your child with is the obvious requirement BEFORE leaving your child with anyone.

- **Get references** from other parents for baby sitters.

- **Invite the person over** while you are home and watch how your child is treated.

- Get to **meet the family of the baby sitter** BEFORE you leave your child.

- Make sure there are **emergency back-ups** for your babysitter. Leave names and phone numbers of relatives, neighbors, etc.

- If you are going to leave your child in the house of another family, even though they may be your relatives, be sure that they family and their friends are good people whom you can trust.

- Make sure that the people taking care of your children have emergency phone numbers which would include yours, the pediatricians and other members of your family.

- Make sure there are emergency back-ups if you will be distant from your child.

- **Never, ever leave your child with someone** if you do not feel 100% sure your child will be treated with respect and will not be harmed.

Safety with BOYFRIENDS

Boyfriends can be a safe or dangerous source of care for your child. Studies show that males are more likely to shake babies and young children than females. "Shaken Baby Syndrome" is the cause of many infant deaths.

- BEFORE leaving your child with your boyfriend, **observe how he handles your child** in your presence. How does he respond to your crying child?

- DO NOT leave your child with your boyfriend or anyone else who has a **drug and/or alcohol problem**. Children need caring, stable and reliable people as caregivers.

Safety in PRESCHOOL and SCHOOL SETTINGS

Children spend a lot of time at school. School is like having a job. Because children are going to be around many different adults and other children, here are some suggestions for keeping your child safe.

- **Meet your child's school teachers** and administrators. Make sure they know who you are.

- **Be a presence** in your child's school. Volunteer for lunchroom and playground duty. Become a teacher's aide.

- **Drop in without notice**, especially at the preschool level and observe how the school really operates.

- Check the **"physical punishment" policy** of your school. Make sure you tell teachers that your child is not to be hit.

- Pay attention to children with the reputation of being a **bully**. Does your school have an anti-bully policy in place?

- Pay attention to outsiders or older children hanging around the school and school parking lot. Communities have made schools a Drug Free zone. The school should be free from **drugs and gangs**.

- If your child is involved in **after-school activities**, get to know the teacher. Private lessons can be unsafe situations for children. If you can, be present. If not, ask your child what went on during every session. Unwillingness to talk about the session or not wanting to go back could be a sign that something is not right.

- Make it a policy that your child is **never alone with an adult**. Remember there is safety in numbers!

Safety in COMMUNITY SETTINGS and PEER GROUPS

Knowing where your child is and with whom is critical in keeping your child safe. Here are some suggestions for your child's safety:

- **Travel in pairs and groups.** Once again, there is safety in numbers.

- **Give your child a cell phone.** The ability to get help is critical for your child's safety. And, if the child is going to be late, or if travel arrangements have changed, have your child call you and let you know.

- **Know your child's friends.** Invite them over. Let your house be the place where everyone gathers!

- **Meet the parents** of your children's closest friends.

- Have your child **buddy up**. If walking to and from school is necessary, make sure your child walks with others on main, well lit and populated streets.

Safety from STRANGERS

Safety from strangers is a major concern for many children and parents. While the media consistently portrays the "stranger abduction" as a major source of danger to children, the data show that most children are hurt, abducted or killed by people they know.

- Create a **password** between you and your child. This password is used in emergencies. If a stranger says to your child that her parents have been hurt and she must come with him, have your child ask for the **password**. If the stranger cannot give the password, your child is not to go along, but to run away, start screaming, use the cell phone to check with you or run to another adult they know. **Teach your child that under no circumstances are they to go anywhere with people they do not know.** Use the password.

- **If children get lost**, teach them to "find a mommy" and say you are lost. Or look for

211

someone in uniform like the police or fire fighter, etc and say you are lost. In a store, look for a salesperson or someone behind the cash register.

- **Teach your children to scream, yell, kick, and run if someone they do not know grabs them.** Most children are frightened and go along without fighting back or running away.

Safety from EMOTIONAL HARM

Safety from Emotional Harm especially relates to the Internet, video games, TV and the movies. Parental control is the best way to keep children safe.

- Sexual molestation occurs for many children who arrange meetings on the internet. Molesters use **e-mail, chat rooms and instant messaging** to get potential victims.

- **Harassment and bullying** can happen to a child in person, via E-mail or through cell phones. Such bullying is meant to bother the child, but can cause a lot of emotional distress.

- **Video games that have sexual and violent language and graphics** can confuse children into thinking that such actions are normal. Children learn violent behavior by experiencing it first hand, and also by watching violence in movies, on TV and in video games.

- Parents can prevent emotional harm to their children and promote their emotional safety by observing Internet, computer games and cell phone use.

Safety from SEXUAL HARM

Safety from Sexual Harm is an ongoing concern. Studies show that 1 in 7 girls will be sexually approached on the Internet. Additionally, one in four women and one in six men report having experienced some form of sexual abuse in childhood. There are proven steps parents can use to protect their children.

- **Educate children about sex**, sexual body parts, and sexual abuse at an early but appropriate age in life.

- Most sexual abuse occurs with someone the child knows. **Be knowledgeable of who is with your children.**

- **Teach children to be assertive.** Teach them to use "no" when it comes to unwanted or sexual touch.

- **Teach children personal protective skills** such as screaming, yelling, running away, scratching if grabbed by a stranger.

- **Respect children's bodies.** Use proper terminology when referring to children's sexual body parts.

- **Keep open the communication** between you and your child. If your child cannot communicate with their parents and get factual and respectful communication, then the child is left to other, often-unreliable sources for information.

212

KEEPING YOUR CHILDREN SUPERVISED

Remember, children need to be supervised <u>at all times</u>.

Be aware of where your children are and what they're doing when you are:

- at work
- out with your friends
- on the phone
- cooking
- sleeping
- watching TV

Supervise your children or make sure they have adequate supervision when they are …
- at the mall
- at the movies
- at a skating rink
- at a playground

Don't allow your children to play in an unsafe place or a place with no or inadequate supervision like …
- in an unfenced yard
- at a lake
- in the park

I feel like I can tell you anything Dad.

Notes and Comments:

Family Home Practice Assignment.

1. Hold a family meeting to discuss ways to stay safe from physical, emotional and sexual harm.

2. Discuss where they might find these dangers. (In the car, home, strangers, school, friends, community, internet, videogames. etc)

3. Establish a special password with your child(ren) to help them identify strangers.

4. Discuss how they should react if a stranger tries to approach them. Practice what they should do together as a family.

5. Spend a minimum of 30 to 45 minutes each day playing, reading, and/or practicing nurturing touch with your child(ren).

Chapter 48

Possessive and Violent Relationships

Goal: **_To increase parent's awareness about violent and possesive relationships._**

Possessive relationships are initially confused with love. However, love is unconditional; possessive relationships are conditional. There is a relationship between violence and self-destructive behaviors in teenage girls. One in five girls has experienced physical or sexual violence by a dating partner. Many of these girls admitted to risky behaviors such as smoking, suicidal thoughts and attempts, unprotected sex, drug use, or unhealthy weight control methods. Teen males can be victimized as well. Some teenage girls threaten to injure or even kill themselves if a boy leaves them.

Many girls remain in violent relationships because of the following:

- Girls see violence and abuse as common and normal.

- Girls who have witnessed violence between parents learn that violence is a part of relationships.

- Some girls are unaware they are in violent relationships.

- Possessive relationships turn violent when the girl wants to date someone else.

Issues That Contribute to Involvement in a Possessive or Violent Relationship

- Insecurity
- Low self-worth
- Fear of abandonment
- Power and control
- Clingy attachment
- Jealousy
- Neediness
- Anxiety

Facts about Possessive/Violent Relationships and Teens

- 1 in 5 girls has experienced physical or sexual violence by a dating partner.

- Many of these girls admitted to risky behaviors such as smoking, suicidal thoughts and attempts, unprotected sex, drug use, or unhealthy weight control methods.

- There is a relationship between violence and self-destructive behaviors in teenage girls.

Warning Signs to Look For...

1. Is the boy/girl possessive? Jealous?

2. Is he/she critical of your appearance, physical characteristics, friends or opinions?

3. Are you spending more time together than with friends?

215

4. Are there injuries that you deny having or do you make up excuses for bruises?

Notes and Comments:

5. Do you feel embarrassed or reluctant to talk about the relationship?

6. Are you turning to drugs or alcohol to "forget" about or cope with the pain?

Chapter 49

Smoking and the Dangers of Second Hand Smoke

Smoking and Health Risks

- Although fewer teens smoke today than they did 20 years ago, smoking remains a significant health risk among teenagers.

- Each day nearly 5,000 adolescents ages 11 to 17 smoke their first cigarette.

- Twenty-eight percent (28%) of high school students describe themselves as current smokers.

- Thirty-three percent (33%) of adolescent smokers will eventually die of smoking-related illnesses.

Goal: *To increase parents' awareness of the dangers of smoking to them and their children.*

- White teens smoke more than Black teens with Hispanic teens somewhere in the middle.

- Teens who perform poorly in school are more likely to be smokers.

- Depression seems to be a risk factor for smoking.

Health risks of smoking include:

- Increased risk of heart disease
- Stroke
- Cancer
- Emphysema
- Smoking can worsen lung function,
- Leaving smokers vulnerable to coughing, wheezing and shortness of breath.

- Women who smoke generally have earlier menopause.

- Pregnant women who smoke run an increased risk of having stillborn or premature infants or infants with low birth weight.

- Children of women who smoke while pregnant have an increased risk of developing conduct disorders.

Effects of Second-Hand Smoke on the Health of Unborn Children

- Miscarriage
- Stillbirth
- Reduced lung function
- Complications during pregnancy
- Premature birth

Effects of Second-Hand Smoke on babies and Children

- It has 40 toxic substances, which cause cancer.

- It is linked to lower respiratory tract infections (croup and pneumonia).

218

- It is linked to increased fluid in the middle ear (ear infections).

- It is linked to reduced lung function.

- It is linked to additional episodes of asthma.

- It is associated with cancers and leukemia in childhood.

- When a pregnant mother smokes, she deprives the fetus of needed oxygen and other nutrients. This may result in:

  - Intellectual and behavioral defects
  - Low birth weight

Positive vs. Negative Role Model

To be a role model as a parent means to set an example for your children to follow. Positive and negative has to do with the behaviors that are being modeled. A parent smoking is a negative role model because of the health consequences associated with it.

Notes and Comments:

Chapter 50

Problem Solving, Decision Making, Negotiation and Compromise

Problem solving is a process. It's a way of coming up with solutions and providing some direction. Problem solving is not the answer. Problem solving is the way to find the right answer for your situation.

There are four components of the problem solving process:

Problem solving is something you do to come up with solutions when you have a problem.

Decision making is what you do when you know what your solutions or options are.

Negotiating is something you do when you know what your solution is, but have a difficult time trying to do it.

Compromise is when two people agree to work together on a solution to solve the problem.

Goal: **To increase parents' ability in problem solving, decision making, negotiation and compromise.**

The benefits of using the problem solving process are many:

1. It prepares children to resolve problems in constructive ways;

2. It builds competence in finding solutions to problem situations;

3. It's the way the real world operates. People just hate being told what to do, even if they agree it should be done. Those who command go nowhere;

4. It's a terrific strategy to combat peer pressure; and

5. It builds on a child's creativity and expands a child's reasoning powers.

Steps to Problem Solving and Decision Making

The problem solving process is accomplished by following the seven steps presented:

1. **Identify the problem.** Describe the problem in a full sentence. Be specific. Vague problems cannot be solved, only specific ones. *If there is more than one problem, work on only one at a time.* Some examples of problems could be:

   - "My child doesn't do what he's told."
   - "I get stressed out being with the baby all day."

PROBLEM LINE UP

2. **Determine ownership of the problem.** Is your child doing something you do not approve of, but does not see the behavior as a problem? A problem will continue as long as the people involved do not view it as a problem. Sit with your child and say, "Son, we have a problem. The problem is _____." Your effort at this point is to help the other person become aware of the problem.

3. **Discuss what you have tried.** Talk with your child about the problem, and review past efforts on solving the problem. Remember to use I Statements rather than blaming You Messages.

4. **What would you like to see instead?** This step allows you and your child the opportunity to resolve the problem by substituting the problem behavior for another behavior. Using the phrase "How to" as a beginning is suggestive and helpful.

   - 'How to get cooperation?"
   - "How to find time for myself?"

   This is the hardest step because you have to be very clear about what you want.

5. **List as many ways as you can to achieve what you would like to see instead.** Ask friends for ideas and think of other creative ideas. This is an individual brainstorming process, and you should *let yourself be as wild and funny as you can, because it might trigger other ideas or help you look at your possible solutions in a new way.* Work with your family in identifying solutions to the problem.

6. **Pick out your three favorite ideas from Step 5.** Decide on ways you will try to solve the problem. As a family, decide on things together. Negotiate and compromise with family members, if necessary.

7. **Try your new ideas.** If they do not work, repeat the process beginning with Step 1. The problem may be different than you originally thought.

Negotiation and Compromise

Another technique to solve problems, reach decisions, and to encourage children to express their power appropriately is through negotiation and compromise.

Every parent and child have, at some time, disagreed on which clothes to wear, what food to eat, when to go to bed, etc. Not always agreeing on things is normal. Children have their views, feelings, and opinions, so do parents. Parents expect things to be done a certain way, so do children. A nurturing family will attempt to work out their differences, not fight over them. In just about all cases, both the children and parents are never completely right all the time. Both views are valid simply because they belong to the people who state them.

There is no magic cure to getting everyone to agree on everything all the time. There is a way, however, of trying to achieve a solution to opposing views. Negotiation is used successfully in many situations. Differences between management and their employees, athletes and team owners, and heads of state from different nations agreeing to the terms of a peace treaty are just some of the many instances negotiation is utilized as a process for helping resolve differences.

Negotiation can be used to resolve differences between parents and children.

Let's look at the following steps to see how negotiation works:

1. When asking for something or stating a view, first determine if there is a difference of opinion between you and your children.

2. State your views and what you think the views of your children are. Remember to be confrontive, not critical, and to use I Statements and not blaming You Messages.

3. Ask your children if your impression of the problem, and your understanding of their views are accurate. Listen openly to their views. ***Do not walk away or argue, but listen.*** Remember, their views are equally as valid as yours.

4. Offer a compromise. ***Be sure to take into account their views, as well as your own.*** Keep negotiating until a compromise is reached.

Sample Negotiating/Compromising Dialogue

Step 1 **Determine if there is a difference of opinion.**

Mom: "Son, you and I seem to disagree on what time should be your bed time."

Step 2 **State your views and the views of the other person.**

Mom: "I believe your bed time should be 8 o'clock at night on weekdays. In my opinion, that gives you plenty of time to play and gets you a good night's sleep. However, you feel you should be able to stay up longer to play."

Step 3   **Get clarity.**

    Mom: "Is this right?"

    Son: "Yes, I want to stay up longer and play."

Step 4   **Compromise**

    Mom: "Alright, let's compromise. You can stay up a little later."

    Son: "How about 9 o'clock?"

    Mom: "Too late. How about if we both compromise and say 8:30 p.m.?"

    Son: "OK, It's a deal."

Watch Out for Compromising Your Values

Family values like no hitting, telling the truth, being honest, etc. are not issues you want to compromise. Personal integrity is something you have to live with. If you compromise what you believe in, ultimately your anger will come through.

Family Home Practice Assignment

1. Practice problem solving and decision making.

2. Practice negotiation and compromise.

3. Spend a minimum of 30-45 minutes each day playing, reading, and/or massaging your child(ren).

Notes and Comments:

Problem Solving and Decision Making Exercise

1. What is the problem? _____

    _____

2. Whose problem is it? _____

3. What have your tried? _____

    _____

    _____

4. Write down the goal statement – what do you want to see instead? _____

    _____

    _____

    _____

    _____

5. List ways to achieve the goal statement:

    a. _____

    b. _____

    c. _____

    d. _____

    e. _____

    f. _____

6. Pick out three of your favorite ideas from the list above: _____

    _____

    _____

    _____

7. Try your new ideas. If the problem remains, go back to the problem statement and the goal statement and check for accuracy. Is the problem you identified really the problem, or is there another problem?

8. Spend of minimum of 30-45 minutes each day playing, reading, and/or massaging your child(ren).